From Doer to Leader:

The Art of Delegating with Impact

Preface

Welcome to "From Doer to Leader: The Art of Delegating with Impact." In this book, we embark on a journey that explores the transformative power of delegation, guiding you from being an individual contributor to becoming a skilled leader who can drive success through effective delegation.

As leaders, managers, and aspiring professionals, we often find ourselves swamped with an overwhelming workload, struggling to balance the demands of day-to-day tasks with the pursuit of long-term goals. We may possess the drive, knowledge, and expertise to make a difference, but our potential remains limited if we attempt to tackle everything on our own.

This book seeks to unlock the untapped potential that lies in mastering the art of delegation. We believe that delegation is not merely about offloading tasks to others; it is a profound leadership skill that empowers individuals, fosters growth, and cultivates a thriving culture of collaboration. By embracing delegation, you can elevate your team's capabilities, foster creativity, and achieve remarkable outcomes that go beyond what any individual could achieve in isolation.

In "From Doer to Leader: The Art of Delegating with Impact," we explore the essential aspects of delegation, from understanding its true essence to overcoming the challenges that often deter us from embracing this invaluable practice. We delve into the strategies that help you identify the right tasks for delegation and select the ideal team members to entrust with critical responsibilities. Moreover, we equip you with the communication tools to convey expectations clearly and provide unwavering support to your team.

Throughout this book, we share practical tips, real-life case studies, and illuminating examples from successful leaders who have harnessed the power of delegation to bring about transformative change. You'll gain insights into how effective delegation fosters an environment of trust, propels innovation, and lays the foundation for personal and organizational growth.

As you read each chapter, we encourage you to reflect on your own experiences, challenges, and aspirations as a leader. The exercises and reflection questions provided will help you internalize the concepts and apply them to your unique circumstances.

It is our hope that "From Doer to Leader: The Art of Delegating with Impact" will not only empower you to excel in your professional endeavors but also inspire you to lead with purpose, empathy, and a profound commitment to the success of those around you. Together, we can cultivate a new era of collaborative leadership that elevates individuals, teams, and organizations to unprecedented heights of achievement.

Thank you for joining us on this enlightening journey. Let us now embark on the path to becoming impactful leaders through the art of delegation.

Warm regards,

Mohd Arif

Introduction

In the fast-paced and interconnected world of today, the demands on leaders are greater than ever before. As managers, entrepreneurs, and professionals, we often find ourselves juggling numerous responsibilities, striving to achieve ambitious goals, and seeking ways to make a lasting impact on our teams and organizations. Yet, the more we take on, the more we risk spreading ourselves too thin, hindered by the limitations of time, energy, and expertise.

In the pursuit of excellence, we must recognize that true leadership extends beyond individual capabilities. It involves empowering others, nurturing their strengths, and creating a harmonious symphony of talents that collectively achieve greatness. This is where the art of delegation emerges as a transformative force, enabling leaders to transcend from being mere "doers" to visionaries who shape and elevate the course of their teams and organizations.

"From Doer to Leader: The Art of Delegating with Impact" is a comprehensive guide that explores the nuances, strategies, and profound impact of delegation in leadership. In the following chapters, we will unravel the layers of delegation, its true essence, and the critical role it plays in nurturing high-performing teams.

Chapter 1 introduces us to the power of delegation, debunking common myths and misconceptions that often hinder its adoption. We will explore how effective delegation can lead to enhanced productivity, better work-life balance, and the unleashing of untapped potential within individuals and teams.

As we journey forward, Chapter 2 delves into the art of understanding delegation, equipping you with the knowledge to identify when and how to delegate effectively. By gauging your team's skills and capabilities, you will be able to discern the ideal tasks to delegate and those best suited to take on the mantle of leadership.

Chapter 3 lays the foundation for successful delegation, emphasizing the importance of clear communication, trust, and accountability. We will delve into the art of setting clear expectations and cultivating a culture where delegation thrives, encouraging initiative and ownership.

Armed with this groundwork, Chapter 4 guides you in selecting the right tasks for delegation. We examine how to prioritize and assess the impact of tasks, ensuring that the delegation process aligns with the overarching goals and values of your team and organization.

Equally crucial is choosing the right people, and Chapter 5 focuses on understanding your team members' strengths and matching them to appropriate tasks. We explore the art of empowering and motivating your team, fostering a collaborative environment that drives collective success.

Chapter 6 dives into the delegation process itself, detailing the steps that lead to successful outcomes. From providing clear instructions and deadlines to offering unwavering support and constructive feedback, this chapter equips you with the tools to empower your team and enable their growth.

However, the path of delegation is not without its challenges, and Chapter 7 addresses common hurdles that leaders may encounter. By addressing issues such as micromanagement tendencies and resistance to delegation, we aim to help you overcome obstacles and facilitate a seamless delegation process.

Chapter 8 delves into the true power of empowerment through delegation, illustrating how it fosters a culture of innovation, creativity, and continuous learning. By enabling your team to take ownership, you will witness remarkable growth and transformative achievements.

Throughout the book, we supplement theory with practicality, and Chapter 9 provides a framework for monitoring and assessing delegation's impact. We explore methods of tracking progress and providing ongoing support, enabling you to celebrate success and learn from challenges.

Chapter 10 delves into the profound journey from being a doer to becoming a leader through delegation. We examine how mastering the art of delegation becomes a catalyst for your personal and professional growth, leading to a rewarding and fulfilling leadership experience.

To offer a concrete understanding of delegation's potential, Chapter 11 showcases inspiring case studies of successful delegation in action. Real-life examples of leaders who have harnessed the art of delegation will motivate and illuminate your path to becoming an impactful leader.

In the final chapter, we conclude our expedition with reflections on the lasting impact of effective delegation. We celebrate the profound transformations that have occurred, not only in teams but also in the lives of those who embrace delegation as a guiding philosophy.

Are you ready to embark on a journey that will transform the way you lead and redefine your impact on your team and organization? Let us now journey together into the art of delegation and unlock the boundless possibilities that await on the path from doer to leader.

Let us begin.

Chapter 1:Introduction

In the realm of leadership and management, the art of delegation stands as a pillar of success. As we navigate the dynamic landscape of modern organizations, the need for effective delegation has never been more critical. Leaders are constantly faced with the challenge of balancing their own responsibilities while harnessing the full potential of their teams.

This book, "From Doer to Leader: The Art of Delegating with Impact," unveils the transformative potential of delegation and its ability to elevate individuals from individual contributors to influential leaders. Within these pages, we will explore the true essence of delegation and its profound impact on organizational growth, team dynamics, and individual empowerment.

The Power of Delegation

At its core, delegation is not merely the transfer of tasks but an exercise in trust, collaboration, and leadership. It is the act of entrusting others with responsibilities, empowering them to take ownership and make a meaningful impact. When harnessed effectively, delegation becomes a catalyst for exponential growth, enabling teams to achieve remarkable outcomes that surpass the sum of their individual abilities.

By distributing tasks strategically, leaders can focus on high-impact initiatives and long-term goals, propelling their organizations toward greater success. Moreover, delegation fosters a culture of trust, where team members feel valued and motivated, leading to higher levels of engagement and productivity.

In the complex landscape of modern leadership, the power of delegation emerges as a cornerstone of success. It is a dynamic tool that enables leaders to harness the full potential of their teams, drive productivity, and foster a culture of trust and empowerment. Yet, delegation is much more than a simple act of assigning tasks; it is a strategic and transformative practice that unlocks the collective capabilities of a team.

At its core, delegation empowers leaders to focus on high-impact initiatives and strategic decision-making while entrusting their team members with specific responsibilities. This distribution of tasks not only alleviates the burden on leaders but also unleashes the creativity, skills, and strengths of those being entrusted. As team members assume ownership of their delegated tasks, they are imbued with a sense of purpose and accountability, propelling them to perform at their best.

The impact of delegation extends far beyond the immediate benefits of task completion. It fosters a sense of collaboration and camaraderie among team members, instilling a shared commitment to organizational goals. This unity, coupled with a culture of trust, cultivates a work environment where individuals feel valued, supported, and encouraged to take risks and innovate.

Delegation serves as a powerful tool for employee development and growth. By providing team members with opportunities to handle new challenges, leaders nurture their skills and build their confidence, paving the way for future leadership roles. The process of delegation becomes a means of mentorship, where leaders invest in their team's potential, creating a pipeline of capable and engaged talent.

Moreover, effective delegation has a ripple effect on organizational efficiency. As leaders prioritize their time and focus on strategic objectives, teams become more agile and responsive to changing circumstances. This adaptability positions organizations to thrive amidst shifting market demands and industry disruptions.

However, the art of delegation also comes with its share of challenges. Leaders must navigate the delicate balance between providing autonomy and ensuring support, fostering a culture where team members feel empowered but not abandoned. Delegating the right tasks to the right people is a skill that requires an understanding of each team member's strengths and development areas.

Throughout this book, we will delve into the various facets of delegation, providing practical insights, strategies, and real-world examples that illuminate its power. We will explore how effective delegation strengthens the fabric of leadership, transforming individual contributors into influential leaders who orchestrate success.

As we journey deeper into the heart of delegation, prepare to discover the art of entrusting, enabling, and elevating. Let us embrace the power of delegation and unlock the potential for extraordinary achievements in our teams and organizations.

From Individual Contributor to Effective Leader

The journey from individual contributor to an effective leader is not always straightforward. Many individuals excel in their respective roles as skilled doers, but the transition to leadership can be daunting. It requires a shift in mindset, a willingness to let go of direct control, and an embrace of collaboration and mentorship.

Throughout this book, we will explore how delegation serves as a bridge on this transformative path. As leaders learn to delegate with intention and strategy, they evolve from being burdened with tasks to orchestrating a symphony of talent, guiding their teams to exceptional achievements.

The transition from being an individual contributor to assuming a leadership role is a pivotal moment in one's career journey. For many, this transformation represents a leap into uncharted territory, where the dynamics of the role, responsibilities, and expectations undergo a significant shift. While individual contributors excel in their areas of expertise, leadership demands an entirely new set of skills and qualities.

In the world of leadership, success is no longer solely measured by personal achievements; it now hinges on the collective success of a team or organization. Effective leaders recognize that their impact goes beyond their individual contributions; it lies in their ability to empower others to thrive and excel.

Becoming an effective leader requires a profound shift in mindset. It entails transcending the notion of working in isolation and embracing the power of collaboration and mentorship. As leaders, our focus shifts from merely executing tasks to creating an environment where each team member can unleash their potential.

Central to this transformation is the art of delegation. Delegation is the fulcrum that propels an individual contributor to become an impactful leader. By delegating tasks effectively, leaders can devote their time and energy to strategic decision-making and long-term vision, while their team members are empowered to shine in their respective roles.

The journey from individual contributor to effective leader is a learning process that requires vulnerability, self-awareness, and a willingness to adapt. It is about understanding and embracing the strengths and weaknesses of oneself and others, nurturing talent, and building a cohesive and high-performing team.

In this chapter, we embark on an exploration of the profound changes that occur when an individual contributor assumes a leadership role. We delve into the challenges faced, the skills to be cultivated, and the mindset required to navigate this transformation successfully. Moreover, we highlight the pivotal role that delegation plays in propelling individuals toward leadership excellence.

Throughout this book, we will uncover the strategies and insights that guide this transformation. We will learn from experienced leaders who have walked this path before, drawing inspiration from their journeys and embracing their wisdom.

Understanding Delegation

Before we delve into the intricacies of delegation, it is essential to grasp its true essence. Delegation is not a sign of weakness, nor is it an attempt to offload responsibilities onto others. Instead, it is a demonstration of leadership prowess, recognizing that the collective strength of a team far exceeds the abilities of any individual.

In this introductory section, we lay the groundwork for the exploration ahead. We will dispel common misconceptions about delegation, examine its myriad benefits, and set the stage for embracing delegation as an art form—a tool that not only achieves results but also nurtures the growth and potential of everyone involved.

As you embark on this transformative journey through the art of delegation, prepare to challenge your preconceptions and open yourself to new possibilities. Together, we will uncover the principles, strategies, and insights that will empower you to become a leader who orchestrates success through the power of delegation.

At its core, delegation is a multifaceted and powerful process that lies at the heart of effective leadership. It is a strategic practice that involves entrusting specific tasks and responsibilities to team members, empowering them to take ownership and contribute meaningfully to the overall objectives of the team or organization.

Delegation is far more than a mere transfer of tasks from one person to another. It is an art that requires a delicate balance of trust, communication, and collaboration. Effective delegation involves understanding the strengths, skills, and development areas of team members and aligning tasks accordingly. It is about fostering a culture where team members feel valued, supported, and encouraged to showcase their talents and abilities.

A fundamental aspect of understanding delegation is recognizing that it is not a sign of weakness or an attempt to avoid responsibility. On the contrary, delegation showcases the depth of a leader's confidence in their team and their commitment to collective success. By distributing tasks wisely, leaders can focus on high-impact initiatives and strategic decision-making, propelling their teams and organizations to greater heights.

Moreover, delegation is a catalyst for individual and team growth. It presents team members with opportunities to handle new challenges, develop new skills, and build their confidence as they take on greater responsibilities. Through this process, leaders foster a culture of mentorship, investing in the growth and potential of their team members.

However, understanding delegation also involves being mindful of its potential challenges and pitfalls. Leaders must be attuned to the unique needs and preferences of each team member, ensuring that the delegation process is not overwhelming or demotivating. Effective delegation requires clear communication, well-defined expectations, and ongoing support to facilitate success.

In this chapter, we will explore the principles and intricacies of understanding delegation. We will delve into the benefits and significance of delegation in leadership, examining how it enhances productivity, nurtures talent, and fosters a culture of collaboration. We will also address common misconceptions and obstacles related to delegation, equipping leaders with the tools and insights to overcome them.

As we journey through the realm of understanding delegation, let us embrace its transformative power and learn to harness it as a force for positive change in our teams and organizations. Together, we will unlock the potential for unparalleled growth and achievement as we embark on this enlightening exploration of the art of delegation.

Chapter 2: Understanding Delegation

In the realm of effective leadership, delegation stands as a linchpin for success. Understanding the essence and intricacies of delegation is vital for leaders seeking to unlock the full potential of their teams and organizations. In this chapter, we embark on a comprehensive exploration of delegation—a process that goes far beyond the simple assignment of tasks.

Defining Delegation: Empowering Through Trust

At its core, delegation is the act of entrusting specific responsibilities and decision-making authority to team members. It involves empowering individuals to contribute actively and take ownership of their assigned tasks. Delegation is not about relinquishing control; rather, it is about instilling trust in the capabilities of others.

At the heart of effective delegation lies a profound act of trust—a belief in the capabilities and potential of team members. Delegation is not simply about redistributing tasks; it is a transformative process that empowers individuals to take ownership, make decisions, and contribute meaningfully to the team's success. In this chapter, we explore the essence of delegation as an empowering force that shapes the dynamics of leadership and fosters a culture of collaboration.

The Delegation Dynamic: A Shift in Mindset

Delegation marks a fundamental shift in a leader's mindset. It requires recognizing that true leadership extends beyond individual capabilities. Leaders must embrace the notion that their success is intrinsically linked to the collective achievements of their team. Through delegation, leaders open the door for team members to step into roles that allow them to grow, learn, and make a tangible impact.

We will delve into the significance of this shift in mindset and the transformation it brings to the leader-team relationship. Leaders who fully grasp the power of delegation understand that they are not merely task assigners but facilitators of growth and development.

Cultivating a Culture of Empowerment

Creating a culture of empowerment is paramount to successful delegation. We explore how leaders can foster an environment where trust, transparency, and open communication prevail. By providing team members with opportunities to excel and acknowledging their contributions, leaders instill a sense of purpose and fulfillment.

Moreover, we address the importance of supporting risk-taking and learning from mistakes. When team members know that their efforts are valued, and they are encouraged to innovate, they are more likely to take ownership of their delegated tasks and deliver exceptional results.

Effective Delegation as a Skill

Delegation is not an innate ability but a skill that can be developed and honed. We delve into the attributes that make delegation effective, such as clear communication, defining expectations, and providing ongoing support.

Leaders will learn how to tailor their delegation approach to the unique strengths and development areas of each team member. By understanding individual preferences and fostering a growth mindset, leaders can create a delegation framework that brings out the best in their team.

The Empowerment Ripple Effect

Effective delegation reverberates beyond the immediate impact of task completion. It creates a ripple effect of empowerment that transcends individual roles. When team members feel trusted and valued, they, in turn, are more likely to empower others within the team.

We explore how delegation transforms a group of individuals into a cohesive unit that operates collaboratively and cohesively. By cultivating a sense of shared purpose and a supportive culture, leaders set the stage for collective growth and success.

Throughout this chapter, we will delve into the foundational principles of delegation. We will understand how it shapes the dynamics of leadership, creating an environment where team members feel valued and motivated to excel. By recognizing delegation as an empowering process, leaders can lay the groundwork for a collaborative and high-performing team.

The Benefits of Delegation: Beyond Task Completion

Effective delegation brings with it an array of benefits that extend well beyond completing tasks. It nurtures individual growth, enhances team dynamics, and elevates organizational productivity. We will explore how delegation liberates leaders from micromanagement, enabling them to focus on strategic vision and long-term goals.

Moreover, we will examine the impact of delegation on team members. It fosters a sense of accountability, encouraging team members to take initiative and demonstrate their capabilities. Through delegation, leaders create opportunities for skill development and career advancement, laying the foundation for a dynamic and engaged workforce.

Delegation is not merely a means to get tasks done; it is a powerful leadership practice that yields an array of benefits that extend far beyond the immediate completion of assignments. In this chapter, we explore the profound impact of delegation on individual growth, team dynamics, and organizational productivity.

Unlocking Individual Potential

Effective delegation serves as a catalyst for individual growth and development. When leaders delegate tasks strategically, team members are given the opportunity to explore new challenges, develop new skills, and expand their knowledge base. As team members take on greater responsibilities, they gain confidence in their abilities, allowing them to reach new heights in their careers.

We will delve into how delegation fosters a sense of ownership and accountability in team members. When individuals feel entrusted with critical tasks, they are more likely to approach their work with passion and dedication. This sense of ownership translates into increased motivation and commitment to achieving excellence.

Enhancing Team Dynamics

Delegation plays a pivotal role in shaping team dynamics. As leaders entrust tasks to team members, they demonstrate a belief in their team's capabilities and foster a culture of trust and mutual respect. This trust serves as the bedrock of effective collaboration, enabling team members to work cohesively toward common goals.

Moreover, delegation encourages a culture of knowledge-sharing and peer learning. As team members take on different responsibilities, they become more aware of their colleagues' expertise, enabling them to support and learn from one another. This spirit of collaboration nurtures a dynamic and synergistic team environment.

Boosting Organizational Productivity

Delegation is a key driver of organizational productivity and efficiency. By empowering team members to handle tasks, leaders free up their time to focus on strategic planning, decision-making, and high-impact initiatives. This enables organizations to respond more quickly to opportunities and challenges, positioning them for long-term success.

Furthermore, effective delegation contributes to a reduction in bottlenecks and delays. When tasks are distributed based on team members' skills and interests, projects progress more smoothly, and teams can adapt swiftly to changing circumstances. This agility becomes a competitive advantage in today's fast-paced business landscape.

Nurturing Leadership Succession

Delegation plays a critical role in developing future leaders. As leaders delegate responsibilities, they are grooming potential successors for leadership roles. Team members who experience effective delegation are more likely to understand the broader context of their work and the intricacies of decision-making.

We will explore how delegation provides a stepping stone for aspiring leaders, allowing them to learn from experience and cultivate the essential skills required for leadership positions. This succession planning approach ensures the continuity of effective leadership within the organization.

One of the most significant barriers to effective delegation is the fear of letting go and the reluctance to entrust others with critical responsibilities. In this chapter, we address these apprehensions and provide strategies to overcome resistance to delegation.

Leaders will learn to identify the underlying causes of reluctance and develop a framework to build trust and confidence in their team members. By embracing delegation as a collaborative and supportive process, leaders can create an environment where team members feel empowered to contribute their best.

In the realm of leadership, delegation is a powerful tool for fostering growth, productivity, and empowerment. However, it is not uncommon for leaders to encounter fear and resistance when contemplating the act of entrusting tasks to others. In this chapter, we address the underlying reasons for this apprehension and provide strategies to overcome the barriers that hinder effective delegation.

Understanding the Root Causes of Fear

To overcome fear and resistance to delegation, leaders must first understand the root causes behind these emotions. Common reasons for resistance include concerns about the quality of work, a fear of losing control, and worries about team members' capabilities. Leaders may also hesitate to delegate due to a desire to maintain their perceived indispensability.

We will explore these fears and delve into the consequences of holding on to tasks. Leaders will gain insights into the long-term impact of resisting delegation, such as burnout, diminished team morale, and limited growth opportunities for team members.

Building Trust and Confidence

The cornerstone of effective delegation lies in building trust and confidence in team members. Leaders must communicate their belief in their team's abilities and demonstrate a commitment to providing support and guidance throughout the delegation process.

We will explore strategies for creating an environment of trust, where team members feel safe to take on new responsibilities. By setting clear expectations, providing adequate resources, and offering constructive feedback, leaders foster a culture of support and continuous improvement.

Setting Realistic Expectations

Fear of delegation often stems from a perceived risk of failure. Leaders must set realistic expectations and communicate openly about the learning curve involved in taking on new tasks. By acknowledging that mistakes may happen, leaders create a safe space for team members to explore and grow.

Moreover, leaders will learn to calibrate the level of delegation based on each team member's skills and experience. By gradually increasing responsibility as team members gain confidence, leaders empower their team to succeed while mitigating potential risks.

Leading by Example

Leaders who overcome resistance to delegation lead by example. They demonstrate a willingness to delegate and share their own experiences of growth through delegation. By showing vulnerability and transparency, leaders inspire their team members to embrace new challenges and seize opportunities for personal and professional development.

Recognizing and Celebrating Success

Celebrating the successes of delegated tasks reinforces the value of delegation within the organization. Leaders will discover the importance of recognizing team members' efforts and achievements, as well as the positive impact their contributions have on the team's overall success.

We will explore strategies for acknowledging and rewarding the accomplishments of team members, encouraging a culture where delegation is celebrated as a pathway to individual and collective growth.

Strategies for Effective Delegation

Delegation, when executed strategically, becomes a catalyst for exponential growth and success. We will explore practical strategies to select the right tasks for delegation, align responsibilities with team members' skills, and ensure clear communication of expectations.

Additionally, leaders will discover how to strike a balance between autonomy and support. By offering guidance, feedback, and resources, leaders foster an atmosphere where team members thrive, leading to exceptional outcomes.

Effective delegation is an art that requires thoughtful planning, clear communication, and ongoing support. In this chapter, we explore a range of strategies that empower leaders to delegate tasks strategically, nurture team members' growth, and ensure successful outcomes.

Understanding Team Members' Skills and Interests

To delegate effectively, leaders must have a comprehensive understanding of their team members' skills, expertise, and interests. We will explore methods for assessing individual capabilities, identifying areas of strength, and recognizing potential for growth.

By matching tasks to team members' abilities and aligning their interests with delegated responsibilities, leaders set the stage for motivated and engaged team members who are more likely to excel in their assigned tasks.

Defining Clear Objectives and Expectations

Clear communication is the foundation of effective delegation. Leaders will learn how to define clear objectives and communicate expectations with precision. By providing a comprehensive understanding of the desired outcomes and performance standards, leaders ensure that team members are equipped to deliver successful results.

Moreover, leaders will explore strategies for involving team members in the goal-setting process, fostering a sense of ownership and commitment to achieving shared objectives.

Granting Authority and Decision-Making Power

Delegation involves more than just task assignment; it requires granting team members the authority and decision-making power necessary to carry out their responsibilities. Leaders will learn how to strike a balance between providing autonomy and retaining accountability.

By empowering team members to make decisions within defined parameters, leaders create a culture of trust and collaboration, enabling timely and informed action.

Offering Ongoing Support and Guidance

Support does not end with task delegation. Leaders must provide ongoing support and guidance to ensure that team members are equipped to succeed. We will explore various methods for offering assistance, feedback, and resources to team members throughout the delegation process.

Additionally, leaders will learn how to create an open and approachable atmosphere where team members feel comfortable seeking guidance and discussing challenges.

Creating a Culture of Learning and Continuous Improvement
Delegation becomes a pathway for learning and continuous improvement when leaders foster a culture that encourages experimentation and innovation. Leaders will discover the significance of providing constructive feedback, recognizing efforts, and encouraging a growth mindset within their teams.

By celebrating both successes and learning experiences, leaders motivate their team members to take initiative and embrace new challenges.

Dealing with Delegation Challenges
Even with well-executed strategies, challenges may arise during the delegation process. Leaders will learn how to address potential roadblocks, including overcoming resistance, handling unexpected setbacks, and providing additional support when needed.

Strategies for mitigating risks and maintaining open lines of communication will be explored, allowing leaders to navigate delegation challenges with confidence.

Conclusion
The strategies for effective delegation presented in this chapter equip leaders with the tools to delegate with purpose and impact. By understanding their team members' capabilities, defining clear

objectives, offering ongoing support, and fostering a culture of learning, leaders enable their teams to thrive and achieve exceptional results.

As leaders embrace these strategies, they discover that delegation becomes a transformative force—one that elevates individuals, fosters collaboration, and propels organizations to new heights of success.

Conclusion

Understanding delegation is the gateway to transformative leadership. In this chapter, we have laid the foundation for embracing delegation as a dynamic tool for empowerment, growth, and collaboration. As leaders learn to trust their team members and nurture their potential, they pave the way for a journey that transcends individual contributions to reach new heights of collective achievement.

Chapter 3: Assessing Your Delegation Readiness

Effective delegation is a skill that requires self-awareness, strategic thinking, and a willingness to empower others. In this chapter, we delve into the process of assessing your delegation readiness—a crucial step in becoming a proficient delegator and nurturing a culture of empowerment within your team.

Understanding Your Leadership Style

Self-awareness is the foundation of effective leadership and delegation. Leaders will embark on a journey of self-discovery, examining their leadership style and tendencies. They will reflect on whether they tend to be more hands-on or hands-off, how they handle decision-making, and their level of trust in their team members.

By gaining insight into their leadership style, leaders can adapt their approach to delegation and align it with their team's needs and goals.

Understanding your leadership style is a critical first step in the journey of effective delegation. In this chapter, we explore the various leadership styles and their impact on delegation, team dynamics, and organizational success.

Leadership Style Assessment

Leaders will embark on a comprehensive leadership style assessment, examining their approach to decision-making, communication, and team management. We will explore different leadership models, such as autocratic, democratic, transformational, and servant leadership, to help leaders identify their predominant style.

Through this assessment, leaders gain insight into their leadership strengths and areas for development, guiding them toward becoming more effective and adaptable leaders.

The Impact of Leadership Style on Delegation

Leadership style profoundly influences delegation practices. We will examine how different leadership styles affect the delegation process, team motivation, and team member empowerment.

Leaders will learn to align their delegation approach with their leadership style, optimizing delegation outcomes and nurturing a collaborative and supportive team culture.

Adapting Your Leadership Style for Delegation

Leaders will discover how to adapt their leadership style to suit the specific needs of delegation. We will explore the importance of flexibility and situational leadership, emphasizing the need to tailor the delegation approach based on the complexity of tasks and team members' readiness.

Through this adaptability, leaders foster a culture of trust and create an environment where team members feel empowered to take ownership of their responsibilities.

Leadership Development for Effective Delegation

Effective delegation goes hand in hand with leadership development. We will delve into strategies for enhancing leadership competencies that directly impact delegation, such as communication, emotional intelligence, and coaching.

Leaders will understand the significance of ongoing leadership growth, positioning themselves as influential mentors and guides for their team members.

Recognizing Leadership Blind Spots

Recognizing Leadership Blind Spots

Leadership blind spots can hinder effective delegation. We will guide leaders in identifying common blind spots, such as micromanagement tendencies or over-reliance on certain team members.

By recognizing and addressing these blind spots, leaders cultivate a more inclusive and supportive delegation environment.

Evaluating Your Team's Capabilities

Effective delegation relies on a deep understanding of your team members' skills, strengths, and development areas. Leaders will conduct skill assessments and engage in open conversations with team members to identify their capabilities and interests.

Through this process, leaders will identify the right tasks to delegate to each team member, ensuring a match between the delegated responsibilities and individual skillsets.`

Effectively delegating tasks and responsibilities hinges on a thorough understanding of your team members' skills, strengths, and potential areas for development. In this chapter, we explore the process of evaluating your team's capabilities, enabling you to make informed delegation decisions and empower your team for success.

Skill Assessment and Inventory

Leaders will engage in a comprehensive skill assessment and inventory of their team members. They will identify individual competencies, expertise, and experiences that contribute to the overall team skill set.

By conducting a thorough skill evaluation, leaders can strategically delegate tasks to team members who possess the most relevant abilities, ensuring optimal outcomes.

Recognizing Leadership Potential

Effective delegation also involves recognizing the leadership potential within your team. Leaders will identify team members who exhibit qualities that align with leadership roles, such as initiative, problem-solving, and effective communication.

By acknowledging leadership potential, leaders can create a leadership pipeline within their teams and cultivate future leaders.

Engaging in Open Dialogue

Open and transparent communication with team members is essential for evaluating capabilities. Leaders will learn how to engage in constructive dialogue with their team, seeking feedback on their skills and understanding their aspirations.

Through open dialogue, leaders build trust and foster a collaborative environment, encouraging team members to contribute their insights and perspectives.

Identifying Development Areas

Leaders will identify potential areas for development among their team members. By recognizing the gaps in skills and knowledge, leaders can provide targeted training and growth opportunities to enhance their team's capabilities.

Investing in development empowers team members to tackle more significant challenges and prepares them for future delegation responsibilities.

Leveraging Diversity of Skills

Diverse teams bring a wealth of expertise and perspectives. Leaders will explore strategies for leveraging the diversity of skills within their team, ensuring that delegation decisions consider the full spectrum of team capabilities.

By embracing diversity, leaders foster an inclusive environment that maximizes the team's potential for innovation and problem-solving.

Building Collaborative Synergy

Synergy within the team enhances delegation effectiveness. Leaders will discover how to promote collaboration and knowledge-sharing among team members, creating an atmosphere of mutual support.

By fostering collaboration, leaders ensure that delegation leads to collective success and a united team spirit.

Analyzing Your Workload and Priorities

Leaders will analyze their current workload and priorities to determine the scope for delegation. By assessing which tasks can be effectively delegated without compromising organizational objectives, leaders can make strategic decisions about where to focus their time and energy.

This evaluation allows leaders to strike a balance between being hands-on in critical areas and empowering their team to handle other tasks.

A crucial aspect of effective delegation is understanding your workload and priorities to identify tasks suitable for delegation. In this chapter, we explore the process of analyzing your workload and priorities, enabling you to make strategic delegation decisions and focus on high-impact initiatives.

Assessing Workload Demands

Leaders will conduct a thorough assessment of their current workload, including daily tasks, ongoing projects, and long-term responsibilities. By quantifying the time and effort required for each task, leaders gain a holistic view of their commitments.

This assessment allows leaders to identify tasks that can be effectively delegated, ensuring that they have the capacity to focus on critical leadership responsibilities.

Identifying High-Impact Initiatives

Amidst numerous tasks, some initiatives carry more significant impact than others. Leaders will learn to identify high-impact initiatives—projects and tasks that align with strategic goals and organizational priorities.

By recognizing high-impact initiatives, leaders ensure that they allocate their time and energy strategically, making room for delegation in areas where it can lead to the most significant outcomes.

Prioritizing Tasks for Delegation

Leaders will prioritize tasks for delegation based on their impact on organizational goals and team members' capabilities. By evaluating the potential benefits of delegation, leaders select tasks that align with their team's strengths and allow team members to excel.

This prioritization process ensures that delegation becomes a value-driven practice that contributes to the team's overall success.

Strategic Time Management

Time is a finite resource, and effective delegation requires strategic time management. Leaders will explore time management techniques that enable them to allocate sufficient time for both critical leadership responsibilities and delegation activities.

By managing time effectively, leaders maximize productivity and create a balance that nurtures team growth and accomplishment.

Creating Delegation Opportunities

Strategic delegation involves creating opportunities for team members to take on additional responsibilities. Leaders will explore how to design projects or tasks that provide growth opportunities for team members.

By offering delegation opportunities, leaders foster a culture of empowerment and continuous learning within their teams.

Delegation as a Tool for Development

Delegation can serve as a tool for developing team members' skills and capabilities. Leaders will learn how to delegate tasks that align with team members' development goals, enabling them to enhance their expertise and contribute to their professional growth.

By using delegation as a developmental tool, leaders nurture a high-performing and motivated team.

Identifying Delegation Opportunities

In this stage, leaders actively seek out opportunities for delegation within their responsibilities. They will assess recurring tasks, projects, and responsibilities that can be effectively handled by their team members.

By identifying suitable delegation candidates, leaders ensure a seamless transition of responsibilities and foster a culture of shared ownership.

Identifying suitable delegation opportunities is a key aspect of effective leadership. In this chapter, we explore methods for recognizing tasks, projects, and responsibilities that can be delegated to team members, fostering a culture of empowerment and growth.

Evaluating Task Complexity and Routine

Leaders will evaluate the complexity of tasks within their purview. Routine and straightforward tasks that do not require their specific expertise are ideal candidates for delegation.

By delegating routine tasks, leaders free up time for more strategic initiatives, enabling them to focus on high-value contributions to the organization.

Assessing Team Members' Skills and Interests

A deep understanding of team members' skills and interests is vital for identifying delegation opportunities. Leaders will conduct skill assessments and engage in open conversations with their team to identify areas where team members excel.

By matching tasks with team members' capabilities and interests, leaders foster a sense of ownership and motivation among team members, leading to exceptional outcomes.

Analyzing Workload Distribution

Leaders will analyze the distribution of workload within the team. They will identify team members who may have capacity for additional responsibilities and seek opportunities to delegate tasks accordingly.

By balancing the workload, leaders prevent burnout and create a supportive environment for their team.

Seeking Team Input

Leaders will actively seek input from team members regarding delegation opportunities. Team members often have unique perspectives on how tasks can be effectively handled and are eager to contribute their insights.

By involving team members in the delegation process, leaders foster a collaborative and inclusive culture, enhancing the success of delegated tasks.

Delegation for Skill Development

Delegation can be a valuable tool for developing team members' skills and capabilities. Leaders will explore how to delegate tasks that offer growth opportunities and challenge team members to expand their expertise.

By using delegation as a developmental tool, leaders cultivate a talented and empowered workforce.

Aligning Delegation with Strategic Goals

Effective delegation is purposeful and aligned with strategic goals. Leaders will ensure that delegated tasks contribute directly to the organization's objectives and long-term vision.

By aligning delegation with strategic goals, leaders ensure that delegation becomes a driver of organizational success.

Developing a Delegation Plan

A well-thought-out delegation plan is essential for successful execution. Leaders will craft a delegation plan that outlines the tasks to be delegated, the team members involved, and the desired outcomes.

This plan serves as a roadmap for delegation and ensures clarity and accountability throughout the process.

A well-crafted delegation plan is the roadmap to successful task distribution and team empowerment. In this chapter, we explore the process of developing a delegation plan that ensures clear communication, defined objectives, and ongoing support for team members.

Identifying Delegation Opportunities

Leaders will revisit the delegation opportunities identified earlier and select specific tasks or projects to be delegated. They will assess the complexity and criticality of each task to determine the appropriate level of delegation.

By carefully selecting tasks for delegation, leaders set the stage for a purposeful and impactful delegation plan.

Defining Clear Objectives and Expectations

Clear communication is crucial for effective delegation. Leaders will define clear objectives and expectations for each delegated task, ensuring that team members understand their roles and responsibilities.

By providing concise instructions and performance standards, leaders enable their team to deliver successful outcomes.

Assigning Tasks to the Right Team Members

A critical aspect of the delegation plan is assigning tasks to team members who possess the necessary skills and interest. Leaders will match tasks with individual capabilities, maximizing the chances of success.

By making thoughtful task assignments, leaders foster a sense of ownership and empowerment among team members.

Providing Necessary Resources and Support

Leaders will ensure that team members have access to the resources and support they need to execute their delegated tasks effectively. This may include providing training, access to tools and information, and ongoing guidance.

By offering the necessary resources, leaders set their team up for success and demonstrate their commitment to supporting their growth.

Setting Milestones and Timelines

Timely completion of tasks is essential for achieving organizational goals. Leaders will set milestones and timelines for delegated tasks, enabling them to track progress and offer support as needed.

By setting clear milestones, leaders ensure that delegated tasks are on track and aligned with broader project timelines.

Establishing a Feedback and Communication Framework

Effective communication is a cornerstone of successful delegation. Leaders will establish a feedback and communication framework that encourages regular updates and provides an avenue for team members to seek guidance.

By maintaining open lines of communication, leaders foster collaboration and enable their team to address challenges effectively.

Reviewing and Adapting the Delegation Plan

A delegation plan is a dynamic tool that requires periodic review and adaptation. Leaders will learn to assess the effectiveness of the delegation plan, identify areas for improvement, and make adjustments as needed.

By continually refining the delegation plan, leaders optimize their team's performance and create an environment of continuous improvement.

Addressing Delegation Challenges

Delegation can be met with resistance and challenges. Leaders will anticipate and address potential hurdles, such as concerns about task quality or team members' readiness.

By developing strategies to overcome these challenges, leaders create a supportive environment that encourages team members to embrace new responsibilities.

Delegation is a powerful leadership tool, but it can also present unique challenges. In this chapter, we explore common delegation challenges and provide strategies for overcoming them, ensuring that delegation becomes a positive and transformative practice.

Overcoming the Fear of Losing Control

Leaders will address the fear of losing control that often accompanies delegation. By recognizing that delegation is not about relinquishing power but empowering others, leaders can embrace delegation as a means of achieving greater results collectively.

We will explore strategies for building trust and fostering open communication to alleviate concerns about losing control.

Dealing with Perfectionism

Perfectionism can hinder delegation, as leaders may believe that only they can complete tasks to the desired standard. Leaders will learn to overcome perfectionism by setting realistic expectations and acknowledging that growth comes from embracing imperfections.

By celebrating efforts and progress, leaders create a supportive environment that encourages continuous improvement.

Handling Team Members' Resistance

Team members may also be resistant to taking on new responsibilities, either due to self-doubt or an unwillingness to step outside their comfort zones. Leaders will explore strategies for addressing team members' resistance and building their confidence.

By providing support and encouragement, leaders empower team members to embrace delegation opportunities and develop their skills.

Mitigating Risks and Setbacks

Delegation involves some level of risk, as team members take on new tasks and responsibilities. Leaders will learn to mitigate risks by providing clear instructions, offering support, and gradually increasing responsibility.

When setbacks occur, leaders will adopt a solutions-oriented approach, using setbacks as opportunities for learning and growth.

Balancing Autonomy and Accountability

Effective delegation requires finding the right balance between granting autonomy to team members and maintaining accountability for results. Leaders will explore how to set expectations, provide guidance, and create a culture of ownership and responsibility.

By striking this balance, leaders foster a collaborative and high-performing team.

Avoiding Micromanagement

Micromanagement can erode trust and hinder team members' growth. Leaders will learn to avoid micromanagement by providing space for team members to work independently, while still offering necessary support and feedback.

By trusting in their team's capabilities, leaders empower team members to succeed on their own terms.

Addressing Communication Challenges

Communication breakdowns can impede delegation effectiveness. Leaders will explore techniques for enhancing communication, such as active listening, clear instructions, and regular feedback.

By prioritizing effective communication, leaders ensure that delegation is a smooth and collaborative process.

Setting Personal Delegation Goals

Finally, leaders will set personal delegation goals to guide their growth as delegators. They will reflect on their progress, celebrate achievements, and commit to continuous improvement in delegation practices.

As a leader, setting personal delegation goals is a pivotal step in honing your delegation skills and maximizing your team's potential. In this chapter, we explore the process of setting delegation goals, tracking progress, and continuously refining your delegation practices.

Identifying Areas for Improvement

Leaders will engage in self-reflection to identify areas for improvement in their delegation practices. This may include addressing specific challenges or recognizing opportunities to delegate more strategically.

By acknowledging areas for growth, leaders open the door to transformative delegation experiences.

Defining Delegation Objectives

Leaders will set clear and specific delegation objectives aligned with their leadership and organizational goals. These objectives may include empowering team members to take ownership of certain tasks, nurturing leadership potential within the team, or improving overall team performance through delegation.

By setting delegation objectives, leaders create a roadmap for focused and purposeful delegation.

Tracking Delegation Progress

Consistent evaluation of delegation progress is essential for achieving set objectives. Leaders will learn to track the delegation process, assessing the impact of delegated tasks on team performance and individual growth.

Through continuous monitoring, leaders gain valuable insights to refine their delegation strategies.

Celebrating Delegation Successes

Celebrating successes reinforces the value of delegation and motivates leaders to embrace further delegation opportunities. Leaders will acknowledge and celebrate the achievements of team members, recognizing their growth and contributions.

By celebrating delegation successes, leaders create a positive and supportive delegation culture.

Seeking Feedback from Team Members

Leaders will actively seek feedback from team members regarding their delegation practices. Team members' perspectives are invaluable in identifying areas of strength and areas for improvement.

By seeking feedback, leaders demonstrate a commitment to continuous improvement and fostering open communication within the team.

Implementing Learning and Development Initiatives

Leaders will invest in learning and development initiatives to enhance their delegation skills. This may include attending workshops, seeking mentorship, or engaging in leadership training programs.

By continuously developing delegation skills, leaders become more proficient in empowering their team.

Adapting Delegation Strategies

Flexibility is essential in delegation. Leaders will learn to adapt their delegation strategies based on team dynamics, project complexity, and team members' readiness.

By being adaptable, leaders optimize their delegation approach for each unique situation.

Conclusion

Assessing your delegation readiness is a pivotal step toward becoming a proficient delegator. In this chapter, we have explored self-awareness, team assessment, workload analysis, and the development of a strategic delegation plan.

As leaders embrace delegation and empower their team members, they pave the way for a culture of trust, collaboration, and growth—an environment where both individual and organizational success flourish.

Chapter 4: Building a Foundation for Effective Delegation

Building a solid foundation is crucial for successful delegation that empowers both leaders and team members. In this chapter, we explore the fundamental principles and practices that form the bedrock of effective delegation.

Cultivating a Culture of Trust

Trust is the cornerstone of effective delegation. Leaders will learn to build and nurture a culture of trust within their team by demonstrating integrity, transparency, and consistent support for team members.

By fostering trust, leaders create an environment where team members feel safe to take on new challenges and embrace delegation opportunities.

Cultivating a culture of trust is the bedrock of effective delegation and high-performing teams. In this chapter, we explore the importance of trust in delegation, strategies for building trust within the team, and the transformative impact of a trusting environment.

Understanding the Role of Trust in Delegation

Trust is the foundation upon which delegation thrives. Leaders will explore the pivotal role of trust in delegation, including the benefits of trusting relationships between leaders and team members.

By understanding the significance of trust, leaders recognize its impact on team dynamics, motivation, and overall productivity.

Leading by Example

Leaders will lead by example, demonstrating integrity, honesty, and reliability in their actions and decisions. We will explore the importance of consistency and authenticity in building trust within the team.

By embodying trustworthiness, leaders set a standard for ethical behavior and create a culture where trust is reciprocated among team members.

Encouraging Openness and Vulnerability

An environment of trust embraces openness and vulnerability. Leaders will learn to encourage open communication and create a space where team members feel safe to share their thoughts, ideas, and concerns.

By valuing and respecting diverse perspectives, leaders foster a culture of trust where collaboration and innovation flourish.

Delivering on Commitments

Reliability is a key aspect of building trust. Leaders will explore strategies for delivering on commitments and ensuring that promises made are fulfilled.

By following through on commitments, leaders instill confidence and reliability among team members, strengthening the foundation of trust.

Providing Autonomy and Empowerment

Trusting team members with autonomy and decision-making power is a significant demonstration of confidence. Leaders will explore the art of delegating responsibility and empowering team members to make decisions within defined parameters.

By providing autonomy, leaders show their trust in their team's capabilities, boosting motivation and fostering a sense of ownership.

Supporting Growth and Learning

Supporting team members' growth and learning is an essential aspect of trust-building. Leaders will explore strategies for providing coaching, training, and development opportunities to help team members thrive in their roles.

By investing in their team's growth, leaders show their commitment to their team's success and well-being.

Acknowledging and Learning from Mistakes

Mistakes are an inevitable part of any endeavor. Leaders will create an environment where mistakes are seen as learning opportunities, not sources of blame or punishment.

By acknowledging and learning from mistakes, leaders foster a culture of continuous improvement and resilience.

Promoting Open Communication

Effective communication is vital for successful delegation. Leaders will explore techniques for promoting open communication within their team, such as active listening, regular feedback sessions, and encouraging questions and suggestions.

By fostering open communication, leaders ensure that team members have a clear understanding of delegated tasks and can seek support when needed.

Open communication is the lifeblood of effective delegation and a thriving team. In this chapter, we explore the importance of promoting open communication, techniques for fostering transparent dialogue, and the transformative impact of honest and respectful communication.

Recognizing the Value of Open Communication

Leaders will explore the value of open communication in delegation, team collaboration, and overall organizational success. We will highlight the benefits of creating an environment where team members feel comfortable sharing ideas, concerns, and feedback.

By recognizing the value of open communication, leaders prioritize transparent dialogue within their team.

Creating a Safe Space for Communication

Leaders will learn to create a safe and non-judgmental space where team members feel encouraged to speak up. We will explore strategies for active listening, empathy, and being receptive to diverse perspectives.

By creating a safe space for communication, leaders foster trust and psychological safety within their team.

Encouraging Two-Way Feedback

Feedback is a vital component of open communication. Leaders will explore techniques for providing constructive feedback to team members while also encouraging team members to offer feedback to leaders.

By embracing two-way feedback, leaders create a culture of continuous improvement and mutual growth.

Communicating Clear Expectations

Clear communication of expectations is essential for delegation success. Leaders will learn to articulate expectations, roles, and responsibilities, ensuring that team members have a thorough understanding of their delegated tasks.

By communicating clear expectations, leaders set their team up for success and minimize misunderstandings.

Regular Check-Ins and Progress Updates

Regular check-ins and progress updates keep communication channels open throughout the delegation process. Leaders will explore how to conduct effective check-ins, offering support and guidance to team members as needed.

By staying connected and informed, leaders foster a collaborative and engaged team.

Handling Difficult Conversations

Difficult conversations are a natural part of open communication. Leaders will develop strategies for approaching and navigating difficult conversations with empathy and professionalism.

By handling difficult conversations with care, leaders maintain trust and strengthen team relationships.

Embracing Diversity and Inclusion

Open communication embraces diverse perspectives and fosters inclusion. Leaders will explore the value of diversity in problem-solving and decision-making and encourage team members to share their unique insights.

By embracing diversity, leaders create a culture of innovation and creativity.

Developing Coaching and Mentoring Skills

Leaders will enhance their coaching and mentoring skills to guide team members throughout the delegation process. By offering constructive feedback, providing guidance, and encouraging continuous learning, leaders empower their team to excel in their delegated responsibilities.

Chapter: Developing Coaching and Mentoring Skills

Coaching and mentoring skills are essential tools for empowering team members and maximizing the impact of delegation. In this chapter, we explore the art of coaching and mentoring, techniques for guiding team members' growth, and the transformative effect of these skills on delegation outcomes.

Understanding the Role of Coaching and Mentoring

Leaders will grasp the significance of coaching and mentoring in delegation, team development, and fostering leadership potential. We will explore the unique roles of coaching and mentoring and how they complement each other in supporting team members' growth.

By understanding the value of coaching and mentoring, leaders can effectively apply these skills in their delegation practices.

Creating a Supportive Coaching Environment

Leaders will learn to create a supportive coaching environment that encourages open dialogue, trust, and growth. We will explore strategies for active listening, asking powerful questions, and providing constructive feedback.

By creating a supportive coaching environment, leaders empower team members to overcome challenges and excel in their delegated responsibilities.

Setting Developmental Goals

Coaching and mentoring are goal-oriented practices. Leaders will learn to set developmental goals in collaboration with team members, aligning these goals with the team members' aspirations and delegation opportunities.

By setting developmental goals, leaders tailor coaching and mentoring to individual needs and growth trajectories.

Providing Constructive Feedback

Constructive feedback is a core component of coaching and mentoring. Leaders will explore techniques for delivering feedback that inspires growth and fosters a culture of continuous improvement.

By providing constructive feedback, leaders enable team members to enhance their skills and tackle new challenges with confidence.

Recognizing Strengths and Areas for Improvement

Coaching and mentoring involve recognizing team members' strengths and identifying areas for improvement. Leaders will learn to leverage strengths to their fullest potential while supporting team members in overcoming development areas.

By recognizing and leveraging strengths, leaders build a team that complements each other's abilities and collectively achieves outstanding results.

Emphasizing Growth and Learning Opportunities

Coaching and mentoring focus on growth and learning. Leaders will explore strategies for providing learning opportunities, such as workshops, training programs, and skill-building activities.

By emphasizing growth and learning, leaders nurture a culture of continuous development and curiosity.

Creating Leadership Pathways

Mentoring plays a pivotal role in creating leadership pathways within the team. Leaders will explore techniques for identifying leadership potential and providing mentorship to team members aspiring to leadership roles.

By creating leadership pathways, leaders foster a sense of purpose and direction within their team.

Establishing Performance Metrics

Clear performance metrics are essential for evaluating delegation outcomes. Leaders will learn to define specific and measurable performance indicators for delegated tasks.

By establishing performance metrics, leaders and team members can assess progress and celebrate achievements.

Establishing clear and meaningful performance metrics is a critical aspect of effective delegation. In this chapter, we explore the importance of performance metrics, techniques for defining them, and how they drive success in delegation and team performance.

The Significance of Performance Metrics

Leaders will understand the significance of performance metrics in delegation and organizational success. Performance metrics provide objective measures of progress and success, guiding team members towards desired outcomes.

By recognizing the importance of performance metrics, leaders can align delegation with strategic goals.

Identifying Key Performance Indicators (KPIs)

Leaders will identify key performance indicators (KPIs) that align with the delegated tasks and overall project objectives. We will explore how to select KPIs that are specific, measurable, achievable, relevant, and time-bound.

By defining clear KPIs, leaders provide a roadmap for team members' success.

Setting SMART Goals

SMART (Specific, Measurable, Achievable, Relevant, and Time-bound) goals are instrumental in delegation. Leaders will learn to set SMART goals for delegated tasks, ensuring that team members have clear objectives and a well-defined timeline.

By setting SMART goals, leaders empower team members to perform at their best.

Using Quantitative and Qualitative Metrics

Performance metrics can be both quantitative and qualitative. Leaders will explore how to balance quantitative data, such as productivity metrics, with qualitative feedback, such as customer satisfaction surveys.

By considering both types of metrics, leaders gain a comprehensive view of team performance.

Regular Performance Reviews

Regular performance reviews are essential for tracking progress and providing feedback. Leaders will establish a schedule for performance reviews, offering team members guidance and recognition for their efforts.

By conducting regular reviews, leaders keep delegation on track and enable continuous improvement.

Encouraging Self-Assessment and Reflection

Self-assessment and reflection are powerful tools for team members' growth. Leaders will encourage team members to assess their performance, identify areas for improvement, and develop action plans for growth.

By fostering self-assessment, leaders empower team members to take ownership of their development.

Adjusting Metrics as Needed

Flexibility is key in performance metrics. Leaders will learn to adjust metrics as needed based on changing project requirements or team dynamics.

By adapting metrics, leaders ensure that delegation remains relevant and aligned with evolving goals.

Recognizing and Rewarding Contributions

Recognition and rewards play a vital role in building motivation and a sense of accomplishment. Leaders will explore strategies for acknowledging team members' efforts and achievements resulting from delegation.

By recognizing and rewarding contributions, leaders reinforce the value of delegation and motivate team members to continue excelling.

Recognizing and rewarding team members' contributions is a powerful way to reinforce the value of delegation and foster a culture of excellence. In this chapter, we explore the importance of recognition and rewards, techniques for acknowledgment, and the positive impact of celebrating achievements.

The Power of Recognition

Leaders will understand the transformative power of recognition in delegation. Recognition acknowledges team members' efforts, boosts morale, and inspires continued dedication to their delegated tasks.

By recognizing contributions, leaders show appreciation for their team's hard work and commitment.

Types of Recognition and Rewards

Leaders will explore different types of recognition and rewards, from verbal praise and public acknowledgment to tangible rewards such as bonuses or additional development opportunities.

By offering a variety of recognition, leaders cater to individual preferences and motivations.

Timely and Specific Recognition

Timeliness and specificity are crucial aspects of effective recognition. Leaders will learn to provide timely and specific feedback, linking recognition directly to the team members' achievements.

By offering timely and specific recognition, leaders reinforce the connection between effort and acknowledgment.

Creating a Culture of Celebration

Leaders will foster a culture of celebration within their team, where achievements, milestones, and successes are commemorated and shared.

By celebrating successes, leaders instill a sense of pride and camaraderie within the team.

Peer Recognition and Team Celebrations

Peer recognition is a meaningful form of acknowledgment. Leaders will encourage team members to recognize each other's contributions, fostering a supportive and collaborative team spirit.

Additionally, leaders will organize team celebrations to honor collective accomplishments and create shared memories.

Linking Recognition to Organizational Values

Recognition should be aligned with organizational values and objectives. Leaders will explore techniques for linking recognition to the organization's core values and goals.

By reinforcing organizational values, leaders reinforce a sense of purpose in team members' work.

Personalized Recognition

Personalized recognition demonstrates genuine appreciation for individual efforts. Leaders will learn to personalize recognition based on team members' preferences and motivations.

By providing personalized recognition, leaders deepen the connection with their team members.

Continuous Recognition and Motivation

Recognition should be an ongoing practice, not a one-time event. Leaders will implement continuous recognition and motivation to sustain team members' enthusiasm and dedication.

By continuously recognizing contributions, leaders inspire sustained high performance.

Investing in Professional Development

Effective delegation requires continual growth and development. Leaders will invest in their own professional development, seeking opportunities to enhance their leadership and delegation skills.

By continually improving their abilities, leaders serve as inspirational role models for their team members, who will also be motivated to pursue their growth.

Investing in the professional development of team members is an investment in the success of delegation and the growth of the organization. In this chapter, we explore the importance of professional development, strategies for fostering learning, and the remarkable returns of investing in the growth of team members.

Recognizing the Value of Professional Development

Leaders will understand the transformative impact of professional development on delegation outcomes and team performance. Professional development enhances skills, knowledge, and expertise, enabling team members to excel in their delegated responsibilities.

By recognizing the value of professional development, leaders demonstrate their commitment to their team's growth.

Creating a Learning Culture

Leaders will foster a learning culture within their team, where continuous growth and development are celebrated and encouraged. We will explore techniques for promoting a culture of curiosity, innovation, and learning.

By creating a learning culture, leaders cultivate a high-performing team that embraces delegation opportunities.

Identifying Development Opportunities

Leaders will identify and provide various development opportunities for team members, such as workshops, training programs, conferences, and skill-building sessions.

By offering diverse development opportunities, leaders cater to individual interests and learning styles.

Supporting Further Education

Further education, such as advanced degrees or specialized certifications, can significantly enhance team members' expertise. Leaders will explore strategies for supporting team members' pursuit of higher education.

By supporting further education, leaders invest in their team's long-term growth and capability.

Coaching and Mentoring for Growth

Coaching and mentoring play a vital role in professional development. Leaders will engage in coaching and mentoring to guide team members' growth and support their aspirations.

By providing coaching and mentoring, leaders nurture leadership potential within their team.

Encouraging Knowledge Sharing

Knowledge sharing is a valuable aspect of professional development. Leaders will encourage team members to share their learnings and insights with their colleagues, fostering a culture of collective growth.

By encouraging knowledge sharing, leaders maximize the impact of individual development.

Performance-Based Development

Performance-based development ties professional growth to task outcomes and achievements. Leaders will explore techniques for linking delegation opportunities to team members' developmental goals.

By incorporating performance-based development, leaders align delegation with individual aspirations.

Investing in Leadership Development

Leadership development is pivotal for delegation effectiveness. Leaders will invest in their own leadership development to enhance their delegation skills and guide their team effectively.

By investing in leadership development, leaders become better delegators and role models for their team.

Embracing a Growth Mindset

A growth mindset is essential for leaders and team members alike. Leaders will cultivate a growth mindset within their team, encouraging individuals to embrace challenges, learn from failures, and see delegation as an opportunity for development.

By promoting a growth mindset, leaders create a culture of resilience and continuous improvement.

Embracing a growth mindset is the catalyst for exceptional delegation and continuous improvement. In this chapter, we explore the power of a growth mindset, techniques for cultivating it within the team, and the profound impact it has on delegation success.

Understanding the Growth Mindset

Leaders will grasp the concept of a growth mindset, where individuals believe that abilities and intelligence can be developed through dedication and hard work.

By understanding the growth mindset, leaders can foster an environment where team members embrace challenges and view failures as opportunities to learn.

Promoting a Culture of Growth

Leaders will promote a culture of growth within their team, where team members are encouraged to seek challenges, welcome feedback, and continually improve their skills.

By fostering a culture of growth, leaders create a team that embraces delegation as a vehicle for growth and development.

Encouraging Risk-Taking and Innovation

A growth mindset encourages risk-taking and innovation. Leaders will explore strategies for creating a safe space where team members can experiment, take calculated risks, and learn from their experiences.

By encouraging risk-taking, leaders inspire creativity and boldness in their team's approach to delegated tasks.

Learning from Failures and Setbacks

Failures and setbacks are part of the growth process. Leaders will explore techniques for reframing failures as learning opportunities and encouraging team members to analyze and learn from their mistakes.

By promoting a learning-oriented perspective, leaders show that setbacks are stepping stones to success.

Setting Stretch Goals

Stretch goals challenge team members to go beyond their comfort zones. Leaders will learn to set ambitious yet attainable stretch goals that motivate team members to stretch their capabilities.

By setting stretch goals, leaders cultivate a team that continuously seeks growth and improvement.

Recognizing Effort and Resilience

Leaders will recognize and praise team members' efforts and resilience in the face of challenges. Acknowledging determination and perseverance reinforces the value of a growth mindset.

By recognizing effort and resilience, leaders inspire a sense of purpose and commitment within their team.

Providing Support and Resources

Support and resources are essential for nurturing a growth mindset. Leaders will ensure that team members have access to the support and resources they need to pursue their learning and development goals.

By providing support, leaders demonstrate their commitment to their team's growth.

Leading by Example

Leaders will lead by example and demonstrate a growth mindset in their own actions and attitudes. We will explore techniques for showing vulnerability, embracing challenges, and seeking feedback.

By leading with a growth mindset, leaders inspire their team to do the same.

Chapter 5: Selecting the Right Tasks for Delegation

Selecting the right tasks for delegation is a pivotal step in maximizing team productivity and leadership effectiveness. In this chapter, we delve deeper into the process of task selection, exploring methodologies, and considerations that lead to successful delegation outcomes.

Assessing Task Complexity and Repetitiveness

Leaders will assess task complexity and repetitiveness to determine their suitability for delegation. We will explore techniques for breaking down complex tasks into manageable components and identifying repetitive tasks that can be delegated.

By understanding task complexity, leaders streamline the delegation process and empower team members to handle diverse responsibilities.

Assessing task complexity and repetitiveness is a crucial step in determining the suitability of tasks for delegation. In this chapter, we explore methods for evaluating task complexity, techniques for handling repetitive tasks, and the strategic significance of these assessments.

Understanding Task Complexity

Leaders will gain insight into the various aspects of task complexity, including the number of steps involved, the level of decision-making required, and the potential challenges.

By understanding task complexity, leaders can identify tasks that require delegation to maximize efficiency and expertise.

Breaking Down Complex Tasks

Leaders will learn how to break down complex tasks into manageable subtasks. We will explore techniques such as task decomposition and process mapping.

By breaking down complex tasks, leaders make delegation more approachable and set team members up for success.

Matching Skills to Task Complexity

Leaders will evaluate team members' skills and competencies to ensure that delegated tasks align with their capabilities. We will discuss the importance of training and skill development to bridge any gaps.

By matching skills to task complexity, leaders foster a culture of growth and proficiency within the team.

Handling Repetitive Tasks

Repetitive tasks can be monotonous, but they are still essential for operational efficiency. Leaders will explore strategies to manage repetitive tasks, including automation, task rotation, and cross-training.

By handling repetitive tasks effectively, leaders improve team morale and create opportunities for skill diversification.

Identifying Opportunities for Innovation

Assessing repetitive tasks also opens opportunities for innovation and process improvement. Leaders will encourage team members to suggest enhancements and streamline processes.

By fostering innovation, leaders boost team engagement and foster a culture of continuous improvement.

Balancing Delegation with Challenges

Leaders will strike a balance between delegating tasks that offer development opportunities and those that challenge team members to stretch their abilities.

By balancing delegation with challenges, leaders foster growth while ensuring tasks are manageable.

Assessing Risks and Mitigation Strategies

Assessing task complexity also involves evaluating associated risks and implementing mitigation strategies. Leaders will explore ways to proactively address potential challenges.

By addressing risks, leaders minimize the likelihood of setbacks and optimize delegation outcomes.

Communicating Expectations Clearly

Clear communication of expectations is essential, especially when tasks are complex or repetitive. Leaders will learn techniques for articulating expectations, timelines, and desired outcomes.

By communicating expectations clearly, leaders set the foundation for successful delegation.

Evaluating Required Skill Sets

Each task demands specific skill sets. Leaders will evaluate team members' skill sets to match tasks with the right individuals. We will explore the importance of training and cross-training to equip team members with the necessary competencies.

By aligning skills with tasks, leaders ensure efficiency and proficiency in delegation.

Evaluating the required skill sets is a fundamental step in identifying the right tasks for delegation. In this chapter, we explore the process of skill evaluation, techniques for assessing competencies, and the strategic impact of matching skills with tasks.

Understanding Task-Specific Skills

Leaders will gain an understanding of task-specific skills that are necessary for successful task execution. We will explore how different tasks demand distinct skills and expertise.

By understanding task-specific skills, leaders make informed decisions when delegating tasks.

Conducting Skills Inventory

Leaders will conduct a skills inventory to assess team members' proficiencies. We will discuss methods for evaluating technical skills, soft skills, and domain knowledge.

By conducting a skills inventory, leaders gain insights into their team's capabilities and identify areas for development.

Identifying Skill Gaps

Through the skills inventory, leaders will identify skill gaps within the team. We will explore how to address these gaps through training, mentoring, or external hiring.

By addressing skill gaps, leaders build a well-rounded and competent team.

Assessing Learning Agility

Learning agility is the ability to quickly learn and adapt to new tasks and challenges. Leaders will evaluate team members' learning agility to determine their capacity for handling new delegated responsibilities.

By assessing learning agility, leaders can delegate tasks to team members who embrace continuous learning and growth.

Matching Skills to Task Requirements

Leaders will match team members' skills to task requirements, ensuring that delegated tasks align with individuals' strengths. We will discuss techniques for task assignment based on skill compatibility.

By matching skills to task requirements, leaders optimize delegation outcomes and promote employee satisfaction.

Encouraging Skill Development

Leaders will encourage skill development through training, workshops, and coaching. We will explore strategies for fostering a culture of learning and development within the team.

By encouraging skill development, leaders enhance team members' capabilities and prepare them for future delegation opportunities.

Considering Cross-Functional Skills

Cross-functional skills are valuable in delegation as they enable team members to handle diverse tasks. Leaders will identify cross-functional skills and explore how they contribute to task versatility.

By considering cross-functional skills, leaders build a versatile and adaptable team.

Recognizing Leadership Potential

Leadership potential is an essential skill set to identify within the team. Leaders will assess team members' leadership attributes and consider them for leadership-focused delegation opportunities.

By recognizing leadership potential, leaders groom future leaders and enhance organizational resilience.

Considering Time Sensitivity and Deadlines

Time sensitivity is a critical factor in task delegation. Leaders will consider task deadlines and their impact on overall project timelines. We will explore time management strategies to optimize task assignment.

By considering time sensitivity, leaders ensure timely completion of delegated tasks.

Time sensitivity and deadlines play a vital role in task delegation, affecting project timelines and overall team efficiency. In this chapter, we explore the importance of time management in delegation decisions, techniques for handling time-sensitive tasks, and strategies for meeting critical deadlines.

Understanding the Impact of Time Sensitivity

Leaders will understand how time sensitivity affects task delegation. We will explore the consequences of delayed or rushed tasks on project schedules and team morale.

By understanding the impact of time sensitivity, leaders prioritize tasks based on urgency.

Assessing Task Duration and Lead Times

Leaders will assess task duration and lead times to determine the time required for successful task completion. We will explore techniques for accurately estimating task durations.

By assessing task duration, leaders create realistic timelines for delegated tasks.

Considering Task Dependencies and Precedence

Some tasks are dependent on the completion of others. Leaders will consider task dependencies and precedence to avoid bottlenecks and ensure a smooth flow of work.

By managing task dependencies, leaders prevent delays and optimize task sequencing.

Identifying Critical Deadlines

Leaders will identify critical deadlines that significantly impact project milestones or client commitments. We will explore how to prioritize tasks with critical deadlines to maintain project integrity.

By identifying critical deadlines, leaders allocate resources effectively to meet high-priority deliverables.

Allocating Buffer Time

Buffer time allows for unexpected delays and unforeseen challenges. Leaders will allocate buffer time to accommodate potential disruptions and maintain a proactive approach to time management.

By allocating buffer time, leaders mitigate risks and enhance task resilience.

Implementing Time Management Techniques

Time management techniques are essential in delegation. Leaders will explore methods such as the Pomodoro Technique, task batching, and the Eisenhower Matrix.

By implementing time management techniques, leaders optimize their team's productivity and time allocation.

Monitoring Task Progress

Regularly monitoring task progress helps identify potential delays early on. Leaders will establish mechanisms for tracking task status and offer support when necessary.

By monitoring task progress, leaders stay informed and can take proactive measures to prevent delays.

Communicating Deadline Expectations

Clear communication of deadlines is essential for successful delegation. Leaders will communicate deadline expectations to team members, emphasizing the significance of timely task completion.

By communicating deadlines clearly, leaders set the foundation for efficient task execution.

Handling Urgent Tasks

Urgent tasks require immediate attention. Leaders will explore techniques for handling urgent tasks without compromising other priorities.

By handling urgent tasks effectively, leaders maintain focus on critical deliverables while responding to urgent needs.

Analyzing Potential Impact on Team Motivation

Delegation can have a profound impact on team motivation. Leaders will analyze the potential effect of task delegation on team members' sense of responsibility, accomplishment, and professional growth.

By selecting tasks that inspire motivation, leaders create an environment of engagement and high performance.

Analyzing the potential impact on team motivation is a critical aspect of task delegation. In this chapter, we explore how task assignment can influence team members' morale, enthusiasm, and commitment to their work. We will also discuss strategies for maximizing positive motivation and addressing potential challenges.

Understanding the Connection between Delegation and Motivation

Leaders will grasp the direct connection between task delegation and team members' motivation. We will explore how the right delegation decisions can empower individuals and elevate their sense of purpose.

By understanding this connection, leaders can leverage delegation as a tool for team motivation.

Recognizing Intrinsic and Extrinsic Motivators

Intrinsic and extrinsic motivators play distinct roles in delegation. Leaders will learn to recognize and utilize these motivators to inspire their team members.

By aligning intrinsic and extrinsic motivators, leaders foster a culture of motivation and dedication.

Matching Tasks with Individual Interests and Passions

Task assignment based on individual interests and passions can significantly impact motivation. Leaders will explore techniques for identifying team members' preferences and aligning tasks accordingly.

By matching tasks with individual interests, leaders ignite enthusiasm and commitment.

Creating Opportunities for Skill Growth and Development

Delegation offers opportunities for skill growth and development. Leaders will discuss the importance of providing challenges and learning opportunities that motivate team members to excel.

By creating opportunities for growth, leaders cultivate a motivated and skilled workforce.

Encouraging Autonomy and Decision-making

Granting autonomy and decision-making authority empowers team members. Leaders will explore strategies for delegating tasks with appropriate levels of autonomy.

By encouraging autonomy, leaders inspire a sense of ownership and accountability.

Providing Recognition and Feedback

Recognition and feedback are powerful motivators. Leaders will learn to provide timely and specific recognition for team members' efforts and offer constructive feedback for growth.

By providing recognition and feedback, leaders nurture a culture of appreciation and improvement.

Addressing Potential Demotivators

Leaders will proactively identify and address potential demotivators, such as overwhelming workloads or unclear expectations.

By addressing demotivators, leaders prevent potential setbacks and maintain a motivated team.

Fostering a Positive Team Culture

Leaders will understand the importance of fostering a positive team culture where collaboration, support, and camaraderie thrive.

By cultivating a positive team culture, leaders enhance overall motivation and team dynamics.

Celebrating Achievements and Milestones

Celebrating achievements and milestones boosts team morale and reinforces the significance of delegated tasks. Leaders will explore ways to acknowledge team successes.

By celebrating achievements, leaders instill a sense of pride and accomplishment within the team.

Reviewing Past Delegation Experiences

Past delegation experiences provide valuable insights. Leaders will review past instances of task delegation to identify successes, challenges, and lessons learned.

By learning from past experiences, leaders refine their delegation approach and enhance future outcomes.

Reviewing past delegation experiences is a valuable exercise for refining delegation strategies and improving delegation outcomes. In this chapter, we explore the importance of learning from past experiences, techniques for conducting thorough reviews, and the positive impact on future delegation decisions.

The Value of Learning from Past Experiences

Leaders will understand the value of learning from past delegation experiences. We will explore how insights from past successes and challenges can inform future delegation approaches.

By embracing a learning mindset, leaders continuously improve their delegation skills.

Identifying Successful Delegation Practices

Leaders will identify successful delegation practices from previous experiences. We will discuss factors that contributed to successful outcomes and the impact on team performance.

By recognizing successful practices, leaders can replicate them in future delegation efforts.

Analyzing Challenges and Setbacks

Challenges and setbacks are opportunities for growth. Leaders will analyze past delegation challenges, exploring root causes and identifying patterns.

By analyzing setbacks, leaders proactively address potential pitfalls in future delegation decisions.

Seeking Feedback from Team Members

Feedback from team members is a valuable source of insights. Leaders will learn how to seek constructive feedback on the delegation process, communication, and support provided.

By seeking feedback, leaders demonstrate openness to improvement and foster a culture of open communication.

Identifying Areas for Improvement

Based on feedback and analysis, leaders will identify areas for improvement in their delegation approach. We will explore techniques for addressing weaknesses and enhancing delegation effectiveness.

By identifying areas for improvement, leaders continuously refine their delegation practices.

Reviewing Delegation Outcomes and Metrics

Reviewing delegation outcomes and metrics provides quantifiable data on task completion and performance. Leaders will learn to assess task success, team productivity, and overall project impact.

By reviewing outcomes and metrics, leaders gain data-driven insights to inform future delegation decisions.

Adapting Delegation Approaches

Leaders will understand the need to adapt delegation approaches based on past experiences and changing team dynamics.

By adapting approaches, leaders ensure delegation remains relevant and responsive to evolving needs.

Incorporating Lessons Learned into Delegation Plans

Lessons learned from past delegation experiences should inform future delegation plans. Leaders will explore ways to incorporate insights into delegation strategies and task assignment.

By incorporating lessons learned, leaders optimize delegation outcomes and team satisfaction.

Creating a Delegation Improvement Plan

Leaders will create a delegation improvement plan based on the insights gained from past experiences. We will discuss setting specific goals and action items for enhancing delegation effectiveness.

By creating an improvement plan, leaders ensure a proactive approach to delegation refinement.

Task alignment with individual interests is a catalyst for enthusiasm and commitment. Leaders will explore techniques for understanding team members' interests and aligning tasks accordingly.

By nurturing personal interests, leaders elevate team members' dedication to their delegated responsibilities.

Aligning tasks with individual interests is a powerful strategy for maximizing team motivation and performance in delegation. In this chapter, we explore the significance of considering team members' passions and preferences, techniques for identifying individual interests, and the positive impact on task engagement and job satisfaction.

Understanding the Connection between Interests and Motivation

Leaders will understand the direct connection between individual interests and motivation. We will explore how tasks aligned with personal passions inspire a deeper sense of purpose and commitment.

By recognizing this connection, leaders can leverage interests to drive exceptional performance.

Exploring Team Members' Passions and Aspirations

Leaders will explore team members' passions and aspirations through individual discussions, surveys, or career development conversations.

By understanding team members' passions, leaders gain insights into their intrinsic motivations.

Matching Tasks with Personal Preferences

Leaders will match tasks with team members' personal preferences, skills, and long-term career goals. We will discuss techniques for task customization based on individual interests.

By matching tasks with personal preferences, leaders elevate team members' job satisfaction and engagement.

Providing Autonomy in Task Selection

Allowing team members to have a degree of autonomy in task selection fosters a sense of ownership. Leaders will explore ways to offer choices while ensuring alignment with overall team objectives.

By providing autonomy, leaders empower team members to take ownership of their delegated responsibilities.

Offering Growth Opportunities

Task alignment with individual interests also offers growth opportunities. Leaders will discuss how delegation can be used to develop new skills and expand career horizons.

By offering growth opportunities, leaders nurture a culture of continuous learning and professional development.

Creating Cross-Functional Experiences

Leaders will create cross-functional experiences that enable team members to work on diverse tasks. We will explore the benefits of cross-functional exposure for skill diversification.

By creating cross-functional experiences, leaders foster well-rounded and versatile team members.

Encouraging Open Communication

Open communication about interests and preferences is crucial. Leaders will establish a culture where team members feel comfortable expressing their passions and career aspirations.

By encouraging open communication, leaders gain valuable insights and strengthen team connections.

Recognizing Individual Contributions

Leaders will recognize and celebrate team members' contributions aligned with their interests. We will explore the importance of acknowledging efforts and accomplishments.

By recognizing individual contributions, leaders reinforce the value of task alignment and team members' unique contributions.

Maintaining Flexibility in Task Allocation

Leaders will maintain flexibility in task allocation to accommodate changing interests and aspirations. We will discuss how to adapt delegation strategies as team members' preferences evolve.

By staying flexible, leaders sustain motivation and commitment in delegation.

Assessing Resource Availability

Leaders will assess resource availability, including technology, budget, and support, to ensure that delegated tasks can be executed effectively.

By providing adequate resources, leaders set their team up for delegation success.

Assessing resource availability is a crucial step in effective task delegation. In this chapter, we explore the significance of resource evaluation, techniques for identifying available resources, and the impact of resource allocation on delegation success.

Understanding Resource Availability

Leaders will understand the various types of resources required for task execution, including human resources, financial resources, technology, and materials.

By understanding resource availability, leaders can ensure that delegated tasks are feasible and well-supported.

Identifying Human Resource Capacity

Assessing the human resource capacity involves evaluating team members' availability, workload, and skill sets. Leaders will explore techniques for determining team members' bandwidth for additional tasks.

By identifying human resource capacity, leaders avoid overburdening team members and optimize task distribution.

Assessing Financial and Budgetary Constraints

Leaders will evaluate financial resources and budgetary constraints to ensure that delegated tasks align with available funding.

By assessing financial constraints, leaders make financially responsible delegation decisions.

Evaluating Technology and Infrastructure

Technology and infrastructure play a critical role in task execution. Leaders will assess the availability and suitability of technology required for delegated tasks.

By evaluating technology and infrastructure, leaders enable efficient task completion.

Ensuring Access to Necessary Materials

Certain tasks may require specific materials or resources. Leaders will ensure that team members have access to necessary materials to perform their delegated responsibilities effectively.

By providing access to materials, leaders prevent delays and obstacles in task execution.

Considering Training and Skill Development Needs

Leaders will consider the training and skill development needs of team members to equip them with the expertise required for delegated tasks.

By addressing training needs, leaders enhance team members' capabilities and confidence.

Dealing with Resource Constraints

Resource constraints may arise during the delegation process. Leaders will explore strategies for dealing with limited resources, such as reallocating tasks or seeking additional support.

By managing resource constraints, leaders maintain delegation momentum and adapt to changing circumstances.

Prioritizing Resource Allocation

Leaders will prioritize resource allocation based on the criticality of tasks and the potential impact on project outcomes.

By prioritizing resource allocation, leaders ensure that essential tasks receive adequate support.

Collaborating with Stakeholders

Collaboration with stakeholders, such as other teams or departments, is essential for resource sharing and mutual support. Leaders will explore ways to foster collaboration to optimize resource utilization.

By collaborating with stakeholders, leaders create a cohesive and interconnected work environment.

Considering Impact on Leadership Focus

Delegation decisions also impact leaders' focus and priorities. Leaders will consider how task selection influences their capacity to focus on strategic leadership initiatives.

By balancing delegation with leadership focus, leaders enhance their ability to drive organizational growth.

Considering the impact on leadership focus is essential in effective task delegation. In this chapter, we explore the significance of delegation decisions on leaders' focus, techniques for managing leadership priorities, and the strategic benefits of maintaining a balanced focus.

Understanding the Relationship Between Delegation and Leadership Focus

Leaders will understand how delegation impacts their focus and capacity to lead strategically. We will explore the trade-offs between hands-on involvement and strategic leadership.

By understanding this relationship, leaders can strike a balance between delegation and personal involvement.

Assessing Leadership Strengths and Development Areas

Leaders will assess their strengths and development areas to determine which tasks are best suited for delegation. We will explore techniques for identifying areas where delegation can enhance leadership growth.

By focusing on their strengths, leaders optimize their contributions to the team.

Setting Clear Leadership Priorities

Leaders will set clear leadership priorities aligned with organizational objectives. We will discuss how effective delegation allows leaders to focus on high-impact initiatives.

By setting priorities, leaders avoid distractions and maintain a strategic focus.

Delegating Non-Core Activities

Leaders will identify non-core activities that can be delegated to team members. We will explore how delegation of non-core tasks frees up time for leaders to concentrate on core responsibilities.

By delegating non-core activities, leaders streamline their focus on critical matters.

Balancing Delegation with Hands-On Involvement

Balancing delegation with hands-on involvement is essential. Leaders will explore techniques for maintaining involvement without micromanaging.

By balancing delegation, leaders foster a culture of trust and empowerment.

Effective Communication and Reporting

Leaders will establish effective communication and reporting mechanisms to stay informed without being overly involved in day-to-day details.

By optimizing communication, leaders can stay updated while maintaining their focus on strategic priorities.

Strategic Time Management

Leaders will learn strategic time management techniques to allocate time to strategic tasks, delegation, and personal development.

By managing time strategically, leaders maximize their impact and effectiveness.

Continuous Improvement and Adaptation

Leaders will embrace continuous improvement and adaptation in their delegation approach. We will explore how flexibility and responsiveness contribute to better leadership focus.

By adapting delegation practices, leaders continuously enhance their leadership effectiveness.

Measuring Leadership Impact

Leaders will explore ways to measure their leadership impact on both delegated tasks and strategic initiatives. We will discuss metrics for leadership effectiveness.

By measuring impact, leaders gain insights into their contributions and make informed leadership decisions.

Conclusion

Selecting the right tasks for delegation is a strategic process that encompasses task complexity, skill alignment, time sensitivity, and team motivation. In this chapter, leaders assess past experiences, consider resource availability, and align tasks with individual interests.

By making informed task selection decisions, leaders empower their team, elevate team motivation, and amplify the impact of delegation on overall organizational success.

Chapter 6: Choosing the Right People

Choosing the right people for delegated tasks is a fundamental aspect of successful task distribution. In this chapter, we explore the process of selecting suitable team members, techniques for assessing capabilities, and the strategic impact of making well-informed delegation decisions.

Understanding the Importance of Selection

Leaders will understand the critical importance of choosing the right people for delegated tasks. We will explore how selecting the right individuals can enhance task efficiency and team productivity.

By valuing selection, leaders set the foundation for delegation success.

Understanding the importance of selection is a fundamental aspect of effective task delegation. In this chapter, we delve into the significance of selecting the right individuals for delegated tasks, the impact of selection on team dynamics, and the strategic benefits of making informed selection decisions.

Enabling Task Efficiency and Success

Leaders will understand how selecting the right individuals directly impacts task efficiency and success. We will explore how matching tasks with suitable team members improves the quality and timeliness of deliverables.

By valuing selection, leaders optimize task execution and project outcomes.

Enhancing Team Productivity

Selection plays a key role in team productivity. Leaders will explore how choosing individuals with the right skills and expertise fosters collaboration and synergy among team members.

By enhancing team productivity, leaders drive overall team performance.

Motivating Team Members

Selection decisions can have a profound impact on team members' motivation and engagement. Leaders will discuss how delegation of tasks aligned with individual interests and strengths inspires a sense of purpose and commitment.

By motivating team members, leaders create an enthusiastic and dedicated workforce.

Fostering a Culture of Trust and Empowerment

The process of selection is instrumental in fostering a culture of trust and empowerment. Leaders will explore how delegating tasks to capable team members demonstrates confidence in their abilities.

By fostering trust and empowerment, leaders encourage ownership and accountability.

Unlocking Individual Potential

Leaders will understand how selection decisions unlock individual potential within the team. We will discuss how providing growth opportunities through delegation enables team members to flourish.

By unlocking individual potential, leaders nurture talent and promote professional development.

Building High-Performing Teams

The collective impact of selection choices contributes to building high-performing teams. Leaders will explore how assembling a team of diverse skills and talents enhances team dynamics.

By building high-performing teams, leaders create a competitive advantage for the organization.

Achieving Strategic Objectives

Selection decisions align with the organization's strategic objectives. Leaders will discuss how task delegation to the right individuals supports the overall vision and mission of the organization.

By achieving strategic objectives, leaders drive organizational success.

Creating a Positive Work Environment

The importance of selection extends to creating a positive work environment. Leaders will explore how well-suited task assignments contribute to a harmonious and collaborative workplace.

By creating a positive work environment, leaders promote job satisfaction and employee retention.

Mitigating Risks and Minimizing Errors

Selection decisions also play a role in mitigating risks and minimizing errors. Leaders will discuss how matching tasks with capable team members reduces the likelihood of mistakes and setbacks.

By mitigating risks, leaders ensure smooth task execution and project continuity.

Analyzing Team Members' Skills and Expertise

Leaders will analyze team members' skills, expertise, and experience to match them with tasks that align with their capabilities. We will discuss the significance of considering both technical and soft skills.

By analyzing skills, leaders ensure tasks are assigned to the most qualified individuals.

Analyzing team members' skills and expertise is a critical step in making informed delegation decisions. In this chapter, we explore the significance of assessing individual capabilities, techniques for skill evaluation, and the strategic impact on delegation outcomes.

Understanding the Role of Skill Analysis in Delegation

Leaders will understand how skill analysis is the foundation of effective delegation. We will explore how matching tasks with team members' strengths leads to optimal task assignment.

By valuing skill analysis, leaders lay the groundwork for successful delegation.

Identifying Technical Skills

Leaders will identify team members' technical skills related to their roles and responsibilities. We will discuss how technical proficiency contributes to task efficiency and quality.

By identifying technical skills, leaders ensure tasks are assigned to the most qualified individuals.

Assessing Soft Skills

Soft skills are equally vital in delegation. Leaders will explore team members' communication, problem-solving, and teamwork abilities.

By assessing soft skills, leaders enable smooth collaboration and task execution.

Recognizing Domain Knowledge

Domain knowledge is crucial for certain tasks that require industry-specific expertise. Leaders will assess team members' familiarity with relevant domains.

By recognizing domain knowledge, leaders optimize task outcomes and decision-making.

Exploring Transferable Skills

Transferable skills are valuable assets in delegation. Leaders will identify team members' transferable skills that can be applied to a variety of tasks.

By exploring transferable skills, leaders foster task versatility and team adaptability.

Mapping Skills to Task Requirements

Leaders will map team members' skills to specific task requirements. We will discuss techniques for task alignment based on capabilities.

By mapping skills to task requirements, leaders ensure tasks are delegated to the most suitable individuals.

Identifying Growth Opportunities

Skill analysis also reveals growth opportunities for team members. Leaders will explore how delegation can be used to develop new skills and foster career advancement.

By identifying growth opportunities, leaders empower team members to reach their full potential.

Consideration for Skill Development

Leaders will consider skill development needs identified through skill analysis. We will discuss how training and mentoring can enhance team members' competencies.

By addressing skill development, leaders promote continuous learning and improvement.

Balancing Skill Complementarity within the Team

Analyzing team members' skills also involves balancing skill complementarity within the team. Leaders will explore how a mix of diverse skills contributes to team synergy.

By balancing skill complementarity, leaders build a collaborative and high-performing team.

Assessing Willingness and Interest

Willingness and interest are essential for task commitment and enthusiasm. Leaders will explore techniques for assessing team members' willingness to take on delegated tasks and their interest in specific responsibilities.

By considering willingness and interest, leaders ensure team members are motivated to excel.

Assessing team members' willingness and interest in delegated tasks is crucial for fostering motivation and engagement. In this chapter, we explore the significance of gauging team members' enthusiasm, techniques for assessing willingness, and the impact on task ownership and performance.

Understanding the Connection Between Willingness and Engagement

Leaders will understand the direct link between team members' willingness and their level of engagement in delegated tasks. We will explore how enthusiastic individuals are more likely to take ownership and excel in their responsibilities.

By valuing willingness, leaders cultivate a motivated and committed team.

Encouraging Open Dialogue

Leaders will foster open dialogue with team members to encourage them to express their interest and willingness to take on specific tasks. We will discuss the importance of creating a safe space for team members to share their preferences.

By encouraging open dialogue, leaders gain insights into team members' aspirations and career interests.

Conducting Individual Discussions

Individual discussions provide valuable opportunities for leaders to assess team members' preferences and receptiveness to specific tasks. We will explore techniques for conducting productive one-on-one conversations.

By conducting individual discussions, leaders personalize task assignments and build rapport with team members.

Offering Task Options

Leaders will offer team members multiple task options when possible, taking into consideration their interests and strengths.

We will discuss the benefits of providing a degree of autonomy in task selection.

By offering task options, leaders empower team members to choose tasks aligned with their interests.

Recognizing Intrinsic Motivations

Intrinsic motivations are potent drivers of task engagement. Leaders will explore how to recognize and leverage team members' intrinsic motivations to fuel their commitment to delegated tasks.

By recognizing intrinsic motivations, leaders tap into a source of sustained enthusiasm.

Considering Task Fit with Individual Aspirations

Leaders will consider how delegated tasks align with team members' career aspirations and personal goals. We will discuss the strategic advantage of task fit in fostering long-term commitment.

By considering task fit, leaders create a pathway for team members' professional development.

Empowering Team Members through Ownership

Leaders will empower team members by delegating tasks that spark their interest and passion. We will explore how ownership over delegated responsibilities boosts accountability and initiative.

By empowering team members, leaders inspire a sense of pride and accountability.

Assessing Flexibility and Adaptability

Flexibility and adaptability are essential traits in delegation. Leaders will assess team members' willingness to embrace new challenges and adapt to changing circumstances.

By valuing flexibility, leaders build a resilient and agile team.

Considering Workload and Capacity

Leaders will consider team members' existing workload and capacity to take on additional tasks. We will discuss techniques for balancing workload to avoid overload and burnout.

By considering workload, leaders maintain a harmonious and productive work environment.

Considering team members' workload and capacity is essential for effective task delegation. In this chapter, we explore the significance of workload analysis, techniques for assessing capacity, and the impact on task efficiency and team well-being.

Understanding the Importance of Workload Analysis

Leaders will understand the critical importance of workload analysis in delegation decisions. We will explore how overburdening team members can lead to burnout and decreased productivity.

By valuing workload analysis, leaders promote a balanced and sustainable work environment.

Assessing Current Workload

Leaders will assess team members' current workload to gauge their existing responsibilities and time commitments. We will discuss techniques for evaluating the volume and complexity of tasks they are currently handling.

By assessing workload, leaders ensure fair task distribution and prevent task overload.

Identifying High-Priority Commitments

Some team members may have high-priority commitments that demand their time and attention. Leaders will explore how to consider these commitments in task delegation.

By identifying high-priority commitments, leaders avoid overwhelming team members with conflicting responsibilities.

Recognizing Skill Utilization

Workload analysis also involves recognizing the extent to which team members' skills are utilized in their current tasks. Leaders will assess whether certain skills are underutilized or have the potential for further application.

By recognizing skill utilization, leaders identify opportunities for skill diversification.

Considering Time Constraints

Leaders will consider time constraints that may impact team members' availability for additional tasks. We will explore how to manage time constraints without compromising task quality.

By considering time constraints, leaders optimize task scheduling and resource allocation.

Evaluating Capacity for Additional Tasks

Leaders will evaluate team members' capacity for additional tasks based on workload analysis. We will discuss techniques for determining how much more they can take on without compromising their well-being.

By evaluating capacity, leaders avoid overwhelming team members and maintain productivity.

Promoting a Sustainable Work-Life Balance

Leaders will foster a sustainable work-life balance for team members by considering their capacity in delegation decisions. We will explore how a balanced workload enhances job satisfaction and retention.

By promoting work-life balance, leaders create a positive and supportive work environment.

Encouraging Communication about Workload

Leaders will encourage open communication with team members about their workload and capacity. We will discuss the benefits of transparent discussions to identify potential challenges early on.

By encouraging communication, leaders build trust and understanding within the team.

Managing Workload Overflows

Leaders will develop strategies for managing workload overflows, such as temporary support from other team members or seeking external assistance.

By managing workload overflows, leaders prevent bottlenecks and maintain task progress.

Evaluating Team Members' Learning Agility

Learning agility is a valuable trait in delegation. Leaders will assess team members' ability to learn and adapt quickly to new tasks.

By valuing learning agility, leaders empower team members to handle diverse challenges.

Evaluating team members' learning agility is a valuable aspect of effective task delegation. In this chapter, we explore the significance of learning agility, techniques for assessment, and the impact of fostering a culture of continuous learning.

Understanding the Significance of Learning Agility

Leaders will understand the importance of learning agility in delegation decisions. We will explore how team members' ability to learn and adapt quickly contributes to task success and organizational growth.

By valuing learning agility, leaders empower their team to thrive in dynamic environments.

Recognizing Rapid Skill Acquisition

Leaders will recognize team members' rapid skill acquisition and their willingness to embrace new challenges. We will discuss how this agility accelerates task execution and problem-solving.

By recognizing rapid skill acquisition, leaders identify key contributors to delegation success.

Assessing Adaptability and Flexibility

Leaders will assess team members' adaptability and flexibility in the face of changing circumstances. We will explore techniques for evaluating their responses to unexpected situations.

By assessing adaptability, leaders build a resilient and agile team.

Exploring Willingness to Learn and Experiment

Learning agility involves a willingness to learn and experiment with new approaches. Leaders will explore how team members' receptiveness to feedback and curiosity drive innovation.

By encouraging experimentation, leaders foster a culture of continuous improvement.

Identifying Growth Mindset

A growth mindset is a crucial aspect of learning agility. Leaders will identify team members who embrace challenges and view setbacks as opportunities for learning.

By identifying a growth mindset, leaders cultivate a positive and proactive team culture.

Assessing Problem-Solving Abilities

Learning agility includes the ability to solve complex problems. Leaders will evaluate team members' problem-solving skills and their approach to handling challenges.

By assessing problem-solving abilities, leaders ensure effective decision-making in delegated tasks.

Exploring Willingness to Seek Feedback

Willingness to seek feedback is an indicator of learning agility. Leaders will explore how team members' openness to feedback leads to personal and professional growth.

By encouraging feedback-seeking, leaders facilitate continuous learning.

Considering Cross-Functional Adaptation

Leaders will consider team members' adaptability to cross-functional roles and tasks outside their primary expertise. We will discuss the value of versatility in delegation.

By considering cross-functional adaptation, leaders build a versatile and resourceful team.

Recognizing a Learning-Oriented Environment
Leaders will recognize the impact of a learning-oriented environment on team members' growth. We will discuss how a culture that values learning facilitates learning agility.

By recognizing a learning-oriented environment, leaders foster a culture of knowledge sharing.

Recognizing Growth Potential
Leaders will recognize team members' growth potential and consider delegation as an opportunity for their development.

By recognizing growth potential, leaders foster a culture of continuous improvement.

Recognizing team members' growth potential is a strategic aspect of effective task delegation. In this chapter, we explore the significance of identifying growth potential, techniques for assessment, and the impact on team development and organizational success.

Understanding the Value of Recognizing Growth Potential
Leaders will understand the value of recognizing team members' growth potential in delegation decisions. We will explore how delegating tasks that foster development contributes to individual and team excellence.

By valuing growth potential, leaders cultivate a talent pipeline for the organization.

Assessing Ambition and Aspirations
Leaders will assess team members' ambition and aspirations for personal and professional growth. We will discuss how task delegation aligned with these aspirations motivates team members to excel.

By assessing ambition, leaders inspire a sense of purpose and ambition within the team.

Exploring Willingness to Take on Challenges

Willingness to take on challenges is a key indicator of growth potential. Leaders will explore how team members' enthusiasm for stepping out of their comfort zones fosters skill development.

By encouraging challenge-taking, leaders nurture a culture of continuous learning.

Identifying Capacity for Skill Diversification

Leaders will identify team members' capacity for skill diversification and the potential for learning new competencies. We will discuss how task delegation can be used strategically for skill expansion.

By recognizing capacity for skill diversification, leaders enhance the versatility of the team.

Assessing Learning Agility and Adaptability

Learning agility and adaptability are vital aspects of growth potential. Leaders will assess team members' ability to learn quickly and adapt to new tasks and situations.

By assessing learning agility, leaders build a flexible and agile workforce.

Recognizing Leadership Aspirations

Leadership aspirations are valuable for succession planning. Leaders will explore team members' interest in leadership roles and the potential for future leadership development.

By recognizing leadership aspirations, leaders foster leadership readiness within the team.

Identifying Areas for Mentorship and Coaching

Recognizing growth potential helps identify areas where mentorship and coaching can be impactful. Leaders will explore how mentorship accelerates skill development and career advancement.

By offering mentorship opportunities, leaders invest in the team's long-term growth.

Considering Long-Term Career Goals

Leaders will consider team members' long-term career goals and how task delegation can align with these aspirations. We will discuss the strategic advantage of career development through delegation.

By considering long-term career goals, leaders promote employee retention and loyalty.

Recognizing Contribution to Organizational Success

Leaders will recognize how team members' growth potential contributes to organizational success. We will discuss the benefits of an empowered and growing workforce.

By recognizing contribution, leaders reinforce the value of individual growth for the organization.

Promoting Diversity and Inclusion

Leaders will promote diversity and inclusion in task selection, recognizing the value of diverse perspectives and strengths.

By promoting diversity, leaders foster innovation and creativity within the team.

Promoting diversity and inclusion in task delegation is a crucial aspect of effective leadership. In this chapter, we explore the significance of diversity, techniques for promoting inclusion, and the impact on team creativity and performance.

Understanding the Value of Diversity in Task Delegation

Leaders will understand the value of diversity in task delegation decisions. We will explore how diverse teams bring varied perspectives, ideas, and problem-solving approaches.

By valuing diversity, leaders foster a culture of innovation and creativity.

Embracing Diversity in Skillsets and Backgrounds

Leaders will embrace diversity in team members' skillsets and backgrounds. We will discuss the strategic advantage of assembling teams with diverse expertise and experiences.

By embracing diversity, leaders create well-rounded and adaptable teams.

Recognizing the Importance of Inclusion

Inclusion is essential in delegation. Leaders will recognize the significance of creating an inclusive environment where all team members feel valued and heard.

By promoting inclusion, leaders cultivate a supportive and collaborative team culture.

Encouraging Open Participation

Leaders will encourage open participation from all team members during task delegation discussions. We will explore techniques for creating a safe space for everyone to contribute.

By encouraging open participation, leaders tap into the collective wisdom of the team.

Exploring Diverse Perspectives

Leaders will explore diverse perspectives during task assignment discussions. We will discuss how considering various viewpoints enhances decision-making.

By exploring diverse perspectives, leaders make well-informed and holistic delegation choices.

Recognizing Unconscious Bias

Unconscious bias can influence delegation decisions. Leaders will become aware of their biases and work towards mitigating their impact on task assignment.

By recognizing unconscious bias, leaders promote fair and equitable delegation practices.

Promoting Equal Opportunities

Leaders will promote equal opportunities for all team members to take on challenging tasks and growth opportunities. We will discuss the benefits of providing an equal platform for career advancement.

By promoting equal opportunities, leaders create a level playing field for team members.

Building Cross-Cultural Competence

Cross-cultural competence is essential in diverse teams. Leaders will explore how understanding cultural differences enhances collaboration and communication.

By building cross-cultural competence, leaders foster a harmonious and inclusive team environment.

Celebrating Diversity and Achievements

Leaders will celebrate team members' diverse backgrounds, achievements, and contributions. We will discuss the positive impact of recognition and appreciation.

By celebrating diversity, leaders reinforce the value of inclusivity in delegation.

Matching Personalities with Task Requirements

Different tasks may require different personalities. Leaders will explore the significance of aligning team members' personalities with task requirements.

By matching personalities, leaders enhance collaboration and task efficiency.

Matching team members' personalities with task requirements is a crucial consideration in effective task delegation. In this chapter, we explore the significance of personality alignment, techniques for assessment, and the impact on task satisfaction and team dynamics.

Understanding the Importance of Personality Alignment

Leaders will understand the importance of personality alignment in delegation decisions. We will explore how matching personalities with task requirements enhances task engagement and performance.

By valuing personality alignment, leaders foster a harmonious and productive work environment.

Assessing Task-Specific Personality Traits

Leaders will assess task-specific personality traits that align with the demands of delegated tasks. We will discuss techniques for identifying traits that contribute to task success.

By assessing personality traits, leaders optimize task assignment for individual strengths.

Recognizing Team Dynamics

Personality matching impacts team dynamics. Leaders will explore how complementary personalities enhance collaboration and communication within the team.

By recognizing team dynamics, leaders strengthen team cohesion and synergy.

Exploring Leadership Styles

Leadership styles also play a role in personality alignment. Leaders will assess team members' leadership styles and how they fit with the tasks to be delegated.

By exploring leadership styles, leaders identify potential task leaders within the team.

Considering Communication Styles

Effective communication is critical for task success. Leaders will consider team members' communication styles and how they align with the nature of the delegated tasks.

By considering communication styles, leaders enable seamless information exchange.

Assessing Conflict Handling Approaches

Conflicts may arise during task execution. Leaders will assess team members' conflict handling approaches to ensure compatibility within the team.

By assessing conflict handling approaches, leaders promote a healthy and collaborative team environment.

Recognizing Motivational Factors

Personality alignment with motivational factors is essential for sustained task engagement. Leaders will explore how understanding team members' motivational triggers enhances their commitment to delegated tasks.

By recognizing motivational factors, leaders inspire a sense of purpose and dedication.

Considering Team Role Preferences

Leaders will consider team members' preferences for specific team roles, such as problem solvers, communicators, or organizers. We will discuss how these preferences influence task allocation.

By considering team role preferences, leaders create role clarity and task ownership.

Promoting Team Member Autonomy

Matching personalities with task requirements also involves promoting team member autonomy. Leaders will explore how aligning tasks with individual strengths empowers team members to excel.

By promoting autonomy, leaders foster self-reliance and accountability.

Considering Communication and Collaboration Skills

Effective communication and collaboration skills are essential in delegation. Leaders will assess team members' ability to communicate and work collaboratively with others.

By considering communication and collaboration skills, leaders enable smooth task execution.

Considering team members' communication and collaboration skills is crucial for effective task delegation. In this chapter, we explore the significance of effective communication, techniques for assessing collaboration skills, and the impact on task coordination and team cohesion.

Understanding the Importance of Effective Communication

Leaders will understand the critical importance of effective communication in task delegation decisions. We will explore how clear and open communication enhances task understanding and execution.

By valuing effective communication, leaders foster transparency and accountability.

Assessing Team Members' Communication Styles

Leaders will assess team members' communication styles and preferences. We will discuss how aligning communication styles with task requirements fosters seamless information exchange.

By assessing communication styles, leaders promote efficient and productive communication.

Recognizing Active Listening Skills

Active listening is a vital communication skill. Leaders will recognize team members' ability to actively listen to instructions and feedback.

By recognizing active listening skills, leaders encourage a culture of attentive communication.

Exploring Verbal and Written Communication

Leaders will explore team members' verbal and written communication abilities. We will discuss how different tasks may require distinct communication methods.

By exploring communication methods, leaders ensure effective message delivery.

Considering Language Proficiency

In diverse teams, language proficiency is a consideration in communication. Leaders will assess team members' language skills and how they align with task requirements.

By considering language proficiency, leaders enable smooth cross-cultural communication.

Assessing Collaboration and Teamwork

Collaboration and teamwork are essential in delegation. Leaders will assess team members' ability to work collaboratively with others and contribute effectively to group efforts.

By assessing collaboration skills, leaders strengthen team cohesion and synergy.

Recognizing Conflict Resolution Skills

Leaders will recognize team members' conflict resolution skills. We will discuss how effective conflict resolution promotes a harmonious work environment.

By recognizing conflict resolution skills, leaders mitigate potential team conflicts.

Promoting Information Sharing

Leaders will promote information sharing within the team. We will explore how sharing knowledge and expertise contributes to task success.

By promoting information sharing, leaders create a culture of collective learning.

Considering Remote Collaboration Skills

In remote work settings, remote collaboration skills are crucial. Leaders will assess team members' proficiency in virtual communication and collaboration tools.

By considering remote collaboration skills, leaders support effective virtual teamwork.

Encouraging Constructive Feedback

Leaders will encourage constructive feedback among team members. We will discuss how feedback promotes continuous improvement and team learning.

By encouraging constructive feedback, leaders foster a culture of growth and development.

Conclusion

Choosing the right people for delegated tasks is a strategic process that involves analyzing skills, assessing willingness, and considering workload. In this chapter, leaders understand the significance of selection, recognize growth potential, and promote diversity and inclusion.

By matching personalities, valuing communication and collaboration skills, and embracing learning agility, leaders create a cohesive and capable team that excels in delegated responsibilities.

Chapter 7: The Delegation Process

The delegation process is a systematic approach to effectively distribute tasks and responsibilities among team members. In this chapter, we explore the step-by-step process of delegation, from task identification to monitoring and feedback.

Identifying Delegation Opportunities

Leaders will learn how to identify tasks suitable for delegation. We will discuss techniques for evaluating tasks based on complexity, time sensitivity, and impact on team members' growth.

By identifying delegation opportunities, leaders optimize task distribution.

Identifying delegation opportunities is the first step in effectively distributing tasks and responsibilities. In this chapter, we explore the significance of delegation, techniques for recognizing suitable tasks, and the impact on productivity and team development.

Understanding the Value of Delegation

Leaders will understand the value of delegation in optimizing team performance and efficiency. We will explore how delegation empowers team members, frees up time for strategic activities, and fosters skill development.

By valuing delegation, leaders unleash the potential of their team.

Assessing Task Complexity and Routine

Leaders will assess task complexity and routine to identify suitable delegation candidates. We will discuss techniques for differentiating between routine tasks and those that require specialized expertise.

By assessing task complexity, leaders optimize task allocation for efficiency.

Recognizing Growth Opportunities

Delegation can serve as a growth opportunity for team members. Leaders will explore how certain tasks can foster skill development and career advancement.

By recognizing growth opportunities, leaders nurture talent and engagement.

Evaluating Time Sensitivity

Time-sensitive tasks can benefit from delegation to meet deadlines effectively. Leaders will assess tasks with time constraints and explore delegation options to ensure timely delivery.

By evaluating time sensitivity, leaders enhance task efficiency.

Considering Team Workload and Capacity

Leaders will consider the current workload and capacity of team members when identifying delegation opportunities. We will discuss techniques for balancing tasks among team members.

By considering workload and capacity, leaders prevent task overload.

Recognizing Strengths and Expertise

Leaders will recognize team members' strengths and expertise in specific areas. We will explore how matching tasks to individual skills promotes task excellence.

By recognizing strengths, leaders maximize the team's potential.

Assessing Interest and Enthusiasm

Team members' interest and enthusiasm for specific tasks are important considerations in delegation decisions. Leaders will explore techniques for assessing willingness to take on certain responsibilities.

By assessing interest and enthusiasm, leaders inspire task ownership.

Exploring Interdepartmental Collaboration

Delegation opportunities can also involve collaboration between departments. Leaders will explore how cross-functional delegation can enhance team synergy and innovation.

By exploring interdepartmental collaboration, leaders break down silos and foster a collaborative culture.

Identifying Repetitive and Low-Value Tasks

Leaders will identify repetitive and low-value tasks that can be delegated to free up time for higher-value activities. We will discuss techniques for streamlining processes and delegating routine tasks.

By identifying low-value tasks, leaders improve team productivity.

Analyzing Task Requirements

Leaders will conduct a thorough analysis of task requirements. We will explore how to outline clear instructions, desired outcomes, and success criteria for each delegated task.

By analyzing task requirements, leaders ensure clarity and direction for team members.

Analyzing task requirements is a crucial aspect of effective delegation. In this chapter, we explore the significance of a thorough task analysis, techniques for clarifying expectations, and the impact on task success and team performance.

Understanding the Importance of Task Analysis

Leaders will understand the critical importance of task analysis in delegation decisions. We will explore how a comprehensive understanding of task requirements sets the stage for successful task execution.

By valuing task analysis, leaders ensure clarity and direction in task delegation.

Clarifying Task Objectives and Desired Outcomes

Leaders will clarify task objectives and the desired outcomes for each delegated task. We will discuss techniques for setting clear and measurable goals.

By clarifying objectives, leaders provide a clear sense of purpose for team members.

Defining Key Deliverables and Milestones

Defining key deliverables and milestones is essential for tracking task progress. Leaders will explore how to break down tasks into manageable components.

By defining deliverables and milestones, leaders enable effective monitoring.

Outlining Roles and Responsibilities

Leaders will outline roles and responsibilities for each team member involved in delegated tasks. We will discuss how role clarity fosters accountability and prevents task duplication.

By outlining roles, leaders facilitate smooth task coordination.

Setting Realistic Timelines and Deadlines

Realistic timelines and deadlines are critical for task planning. Leaders will explore techniques for setting achievable timeframes.

By setting realistic deadlines, leaders prevent unnecessary pressure and stress.

Identifying Required Resources and Support

Leaders will identify the necessary resources and support for task completion. We will discuss how providing adequate resources enhances task efficiency.

By identifying resources, leaders optimize task execution.

Clarifying Performance Expectations and Evaluation Criteria

Leaders will clarify performance expectations and evaluation criteria for delegated tasks. We will explore how transparent evaluation criteria promote fairness and objectivity.

By clarifying expectations, leaders establish a framework for task assessment.

Addressing Potential Challenges and Risks

Leaders will address potential challenges and risks associated with delegated tasks. We will discuss techniques for risk mitigation and problem-solving.

By addressing challenges, leaders facilitate a smoother task execution process.

Encouraging Questions and Seeking Clarifications

Leaders will encourage team members to ask questions and seek clarifications about task requirements. We will discuss the benefits of open communication in preventing misunderstandings.

By encouraging questions, leaders foster a culture of proactive engagement.

Seeking Input and Feedback

Leaders will seek input and feedback from team members on task requirements. We will explore how collaborative decision-making improves task understanding.

By seeking input, leaders promote a sense of ownership and involvement.

Selecting the Right Team Members

Leaders will select the most suitable team members for delegated tasks based on skills, expertise, willingness, and capacity. We will discuss the significance of matching personalities and interests with task requirements.

By selecting the right team members, leaders set the stage for successful task execution.

Selecting the right team members for delegated tasks is a pivotal aspect of effective task delegation. In this chapter, we explore the significance of team member selection, techniques for assessing suitability, and the impact on task performance and team dynamics.

Understanding the Significance of Team Member Selection

Leaders will understand the critical importance of selecting the right team members for delegated tasks. We will explore how matching skills, expertise, and personalities with task requirements enhances task success.

By valuing team member selection, leaders set the foundation for successful task execution.

Assessing Skills and Expertise

Leaders will assess team members' skills and expertise to identify the best fit for delegated tasks. We will discuss techniques for evaluating competencies and matching them to task requirements.

By assessing skills, leaders optimize task allocation for efficiency and quality.

Recognizing Willingness and Enthusiasm

Willingness and enthusiasm are essential traits in team members for delegated tasks. Leaders will explore techniques for assessing team members' interest in taking on specific responsibilities.

By recognizing willingness and enthusiasm, leaders inspire a sense of ownership and commitment.

Evaluating Capacity and Workload

Leaders will evaluate team members' capacity and workload to ensure they can take on additional responsibilities without overburdening themselves. We will discuss techniques for balancing tasks among team members.

By evaluating capacity, leaders prevent task overload and maintain productivity.

Considering Personality and Communication Styles

Personality and communication styles play a role in team member selection. Leaders will consider how matching personalities with task requirements enhances collaboration and communication.

By considering personality styles, leaders foster harmonious team dynamics.

Assessing Adaptability and Flexibility

Adaptability and flexibility are valuable traits in team members for delegation. Leaders will assess team members' ability to adapt to new challenges and work well in dynamic environments.

By assessing adaptability, leaders build a versatile and agile workforce.

Recognizing Leadership Potential

Leadership potential is an important consideration in team member selection. Leaders will explore team members' aptitude for leadership roles and their potential for future growth.

By recognizing leadership potential, leaders nurture talent development and succession planning.

Promoting Inclusivity and Diversity

Leaders will promote inclusivity and diversity in team member selection. We will discuss how a diverse team brings varied perspectives and fosters innovation.

By promoting inclusivity, leaders enhance creativity and problem-solving.

Considering Cross-Functional Collaboration

Team member selection can also involve cross-functional collaboration. Leaders will explore how collaborating with members from different departments enriches task outcomes.

By considering cross-functional collaboration, leaders break down silos and encourage knowledge sharing.

Communicating Delegation Decisions

Clear and effective communication is key to successful delegation. Leaders will learn how to communicate task assignments, expectations, and deadlines to team members.

By communicating delegation decisions, leaders ensure alignment and understanding.

Clear and effective communication of delegation decisions is essential for successful task execution. In this chapter, we explore the significance of communication, techniques for conveying decisions, and the impact on task understanding and team collaboration.

Understanding the Importance of Effective Communication

Leaders will understand the critical importance of effective communication in delegation decisions. We will explore how clear communication fosters task clarity, alignment, and accountability.

By valuing effective communication, leaders lay the groundwork for successful task delegation.

Conveying Task Assignments and Expectations

Leaders will learn how to communicate task assignments and expectations to team members. We will discuss techniques for outlining objectives, deliverables, and deadlines.

By conveying assignments and expectations, leaders ensure a common understanding of goals.

Providing Context and Purpose

Leaders will provide context and purpose for delegated tasks. We will explore how explaining the significance of tasks motivates team members and promotes commitment.

By providing context, leaders inspire a sense of purpose and direction.

Clarifying Roles and Responsibilities

Clear delineation of roles and responsibilities is crucial in delegation. Leaders will clarify each team member's role and their contributions to task success.

By clarifying roles, leaders prevent confusion and overlapping efforts.

Setting Communication Channels

Leaders will establish communication channels for task-related discussions. We will discuss how choosing the right communication tools enhances information exchange.

By setting communication channels, leaders facilitate seamless collaboration.

Encouraging Questions and Feedback

Leaders will encourage team members to ask questions and provide feedback about delegation decisions. We will explore how open communication fosters a culture of continuous improvement.

By encouraging questions, leaders promote a culture of active engagement.

Offering Support and Guidance

Leaders will offer support and guidance to team members as they begin delegated tasks. We will discuss how regular check-ins promote progress and address potential challenges.

By offering support, leaders demonstrate a commitment to team success.

Handling Difficult Conversations

Difficult conversations may arise during delegation. Leaders will learn techniques for handling challenging discussions and providing constructive feedback.

By handling difficult conversations, leaders maintain open and transparent communication.

Recognizing Achievements and Milestones

Leaders will recognize team members' achievements and milestones during the delegation process. We will discuss the positive impact of acknowledging progress.

By recognizing achievements, leaders reinforce motivation and appreciation.

Encouraging Two-Way Communication

Leaders will encourage two-way communication with team members. We will explore how active listening and feedback-seeking contribute to a collaborative work environment.

By encouraging two-way communication, leaders create a culture of open dialogue.

Providing Necessary Resources and Support

Leaders will provide team members with the necessary resources, tools, and support to accomplish delegated tasks. We will discuss the importance of removing barriers to task completion.

By providing resources and support, leaders enable task efficiency and quality.

Providing team members with the necessary resources and support is vital for successful task delegation. In this chapter, we explore the significance of resource allocation, techniques for offering assistance, and the impact on task efficiency and team morale.

Understanding the Importance of Resource Allocation

Leaders will understand the critical importance of resource allocation in delegation decisions. We will explore how providing adequate resources empowers team members and enhances task outcomes.

By valuing resource allocation, leaders demonstrate commitment to task success.

Identifying Required Resources

Leaders will identify the specific resources required for each delegated task. We will discuss techniques for determining the tools, materials, and information necessary for task completion.

By identifying resources, leaders facilitate task planning and execution.

Allocating Budget and Funding

For resource-intensive tasks, budget allocation is crucial. Leaders will explore techniques for budgeting and securing funding for delegated projects.

By allocating budget, leaders ensure financial support for task accomplishment.

Offering Technical and Technological Support

Leaders will offer technical and technological support to team members as needed. We will discuss how access to expertise and software enhances task efficiency.

By providing technical support, leaders enable smooth task execution.

Providing Access to Information and Data

Access to relevant information and data is essential for task success. Leaders will ensure team members have the necessary information to make informed decisions.

By providing access to information, leaders promote data-driven task execution.

Offering Training and Skill Development

Leaders will offer training and skill development opportunities to team members when required. We will explore how upskilling enhances task capabilities.

By offering training, leaders invest in the long-term growth of the team.

Creating a Supportive Work Environment

A supportive work environment is conducive to task excellence. Leaders will discuss how fostering a positive workplace culture motivates team members.

By creating a supportive environment, leaders promote job satisfaction and retention.

Removing Barriers and Obstacles

Leaders will actively identify and remove barriers and obstacles that hinder task progress. We will discuss techniques for problem-solving and providing timely assistance.

By removing barriers, leaders ensure a smooth workflow.

Establishing Task-Specific Support Systems

For complex tasks, specific support systems may be necessary. Leaders will establish support mechanisms to address unique task requirements.

By providing task-specific support, leaders cater to individual needs.

Celebrating Resourceful Solutions

Leaders will celebrate resourceful solutions and innovative approaches to task challenges. We will discuss the positive impact of recognizing creative problem-solving.

By celebrating resourcefulness, leaders foster a culture of ingenuity.

Establishing Checkpoints and Milestones

Leaders will establish checkpoints and milestones for task progress monitoring. We will explore how regular updates facilitate tracking and early intervention if needed.

By establishing checkpoints, leaders maintain task visibility and accountability.

Establishing checkpoints and milestones is a crucial aspect of effective task delegation. In this chapter, we explore the significance of progress monitoring, techniques for setting milestones, and the impact on task visibility and team performance.

Understanding the Importance of Progress Monitoring

Leaders will understand the critical importance of progress monitoring in delegation decisions. We will explore how checkpoints and milestones provide insight into task progress and enable timely intervention if needed.

By valuing progress monitoring, leaders stay informed and in control of task execution.

Setting Milestones for Task Progress

Leaders will learn how to set meaningful milestones for delegated tasks. We will discuss techniques for breaking down tasks into manageable stages.

By setting milestones, leaders track task advancement and accomplishments.

Establishing Checkpoints for Updates

Leaders will establish regular checkpoints for team members to provide updates on task progress. We will explore how periodic updates enable timely feedback and adjustments.

By establishing checkpoints, leaders maintain continuous task visibility.

Clarifying Reporting and Documentation

Leaders will clarify reporting and documentation expectations at each checkpoint. We will discuss how standardized reporting streamlines progress updates.

By clarifying reporting, leaders ensure consistency in information exchange.

Utilizing Project Management Tools

Project management tools can enhance progress monitoring. Leaders will explore techniques for using software and applications to track task progress.

By utilizing project management tools, leaders streamline task management.

Analyzing Deviations from Milestones

Leaders will analyze deviations from planned milestones and checkpoints. We will discuss techniques for identifying potential roadblocks and finding solutions.

By analyzing deviations, leaders address challenges proactively.

Offering Timely Feedback and Guidance

Leaders will offer timely feedback and guidance to team members during checkpoints. We will explore how constructive feedback supports performance improvement.

By offering feedback, leaders promote continuous learning and growth.

Recognizing Achievements at Milestones

Leaders will recognize team members' achievements at significant milestones. We will discuss the positive impact of celebrating progress.

By recognizing achievements, leaders reinforce motivation and appreciation.

Addressing Delays and Bottlenecks

Leaders will address delays and bottlenecks during progress updates. We will explore how prompt action minimizes the impact on task timelines.

By addressing delays, leaders maintain task efficiency.

Encouraging Collaboration and Knowledge Sharing

Checkpoints facilitate collaboration and knowledge sharing among team members. Leaders will encourage open discussions and information exchange.

By encouraging collaboration, leaders foster a culture of teamwork.

Monitoring and Offering Feedback

Leaders will actively monitor task progress and offer constructive feedback to team members. We will discuss how feedback promotes continuous improvement and fosters a learning culture.

By monitoring and offering feedback, leaders guide team members towards success.

Monitoring task progress and offering constructive feedback are essential components of effective task delegation. In this chapter, we explore the significance of continuous monitoring, techniques for feedback delivery, and the impact on task quality and team development.

Understanding the Importance of Task Monitoring

Leaders will understand the critical importance of task monitoring in delegation decisions. We will explore how regular monitoring enables early detection of issues and supports timely course corrections.

By valuing task monitoring, leaders ensure task alignment and success.

Establishing Monitoring Parameters

Leaders will establish specific parameters for task monitoring. We will discuss techniques for defining key performance indicators (KPIs) and metrics for evaluating progress.

By establishing monitoring parameters, leaders have clear benchmarks for success.

Using Real-Time Tracking Tools

Real-time tracking tools facilitate task monitoring. Leaders will explore how technology can provide immediate insights into task status and team performance.

By using real-time tracking, leaders stay informed and agile in decision-making.

Encouraging Transparent Reporting

Transparent reporting fosters open communication. Leaders will encourage team members to share progress updates and challenges openly.

By encouraging transparent reporting, leaders build trust and accountability.

Providing Constructive Feedback

Leaders will learn how to provide constructive feedback to team members. We will explore techniques for delivering feedback that motivates improvement.

By providing constructive feedback, leaders support individual growth and development.

Offering Positive Reinforcement

Positive reinforcement is essential in feedback delivery. Leaders will recognize team members' efforts and accomplishments.

By offering positive reinforcement, leaders boost team morale and motivation.

Addressing Performance Gaps

Leaders will address performance gaps discovered during monitoring. We will discuss how timely intervention prevents issues from escalating.

By addressing performance gaps, leaders foster continuous improvement.

Promoting Two-Way Feedback

Leaders will promote two-way feedback between team members and themselves. We will explore how a culture of open feedback enhances team communication.

By promoting two-way feedback, leaders foster a collaborative work environment.

Recognizing Efforts and Progress

Leaders will recognize team members' efforts and progress during feedback discussions. We will discuss the positive impact of acknowledging hard work.

By recognizing efforts, leaders reinforce dedication and commitment.

Learning from Feedback

Leaders will learn from team members' feedback as well. We will explore how leaders can use feedback to improve their delegation approach.

By learning from feedback, leaders adapt and grow as effective delegators.

Addressing Challenges and Roadblocks

Leaders will address challenges and roadblocks encountered during task execution. We will explore techniques for problem-solving and providing timely assistance.

By addressing challenges, leaders ensure smooth task continuity.

Addressing challenges and roadblocks is a critical aspect of effective task delegation. In this chapter, we explore the significance of proactive problem-solving, techniques for overcoming obstacles, and the impact on task continuity and team resilience.

Understanding the Nature of Challenges

Leaders will understand the diverse nature of challenges that can arise during task delegation. We will explore common obstacles and their potential impact on task progress.

By understanding challenges, leaders prepare for effective problem-solving.

Promoting a Problem-Solving Mindset

Leaders will promote a problem-solving mindset among team members. We will discuss techniques for encouraging creative thinking and innovative solutions.

By promoting a problem-solving mindset, leaders empower their team to overcome challenges.

Identifying Potential Roadblocks

Leaders will identify potential roadblocks early in the delegation process. We will explore how proactive identification enables timely intervention.

By identifying roadblocks, leaders prevent unnecessary delays.

Encouraging Open Communication

Open communication is essential in addressing challenges. Leaders will encourage team members to express concerns and seek assistance when needed.

By encouraging open communication, leaders create a supportive work environment.

Offering Timely Support and Guidance

Leaders will offer timely support and guidance to team members facing challenges. We will discuss techniques for providing assistance and resources.

By offering support, leaders demonstrate commitment to their team's success.

Collaborative Problem-Solving

Collaborative problem-solving involves team members working together to find solutions. Leaders will promote cross-functional collaboration and knowledge sharing.

By encouraging collaboration, leaders harness collective intelligence.

Implementing Contingency Plans

Leaders will implement contingency plans to address unforeseen challenges. We will explore how having backup strategies mitigates risks.

By implementing contingency plans, leaders ensure task continuity.

Learning from Setbacks

Leaders will foster a culture of learning from setbacks. We will discuss how resilience and adaptability contribute to long-term success.

By learning from setbacks, leaders turn challenges into opportunities for growth.

Celebrating Success over Adversity

Leaders will celebrate team success over adversity. We will explore the positive impact of acknowledging resilience and determination.

By celebrating success, leaders boost team morale and motivation.

Continuous Improvement and Flexibility

Leaders will promote continuous improvement and flexibility in addressing challenges. We will discuss how adaptation to changing circumstances is key to overcoming obstacles.

By embracing flexibility, leaders enable their team to navigate uncertainties.

Recognizing Accomplishments and Contributions

Leaders will recognize team members' accomplishments and contributions to delegated tasks. We will discuss the positive impact of appreciation and acknowledgment.

By recognizing accomplishments, leaders reinforce a culture of recognition and motivation.

Recognizing accomplishments and contributions is a fundamental aspect of effective task delegation. In this chapter, we explore the significance of appreciation, techniques for acknowledging achievements, and the impact on team motivation and morale.

Understanding the Power of Recognition

Leaders will understand the power of recognition in fostering a positive work environment. We will explore how acknowledging accomplishments boosts team morale and engagement.

By valuing recognition, leaders inspire a culture of appreciation.

Celebrating Milestones and Achievements

Leaders will celebrate significant milestones and achievements reached during task delegation. We will discuss techniques for commemorating progress.

By celebrating accomplishments, leaders reinforce the value of hard work.

Offering Individual Appreciation

Leaders will offer individual appreciation to team members for their contributions. We will explore how personalized recognition makes team members feel valued.

By offering individual appreciation, leaders enhance team motivation.

Public Recognition and Commendation

Public recognition is a powerful form of appreciation. Leaders will acknowledge team achievements in front of their peers and colleagues.

By offering public recognition, leaders promote a sense of pride and accomplishment.

Rewarding Exceptional Performance

Leaders will reward exceptional performance with meaningful incentives. We will discuss techniques for designing rewards that align with team members' preferences.

By rewarding exceptional performance, leaders encourage continued excellence.

Providing Growth and Development Opportunities

Leaders will provide growth and development opportunities as a form of recognition. We will explore how investing in team members' professional growth fosters loyalty.

By providing development opportunities, leaders invest in their team's future.

Promoting a Culture of Appreciation

Leaders will promote a culture of appreciation within the team. We will discuss techniques for encouraging team members to recognize each other's efforts.

By promoting a culture of appreciation, leaders foster mutual support.

Incorporating Recognition in Team Meetings

Leaders will incorporate recognition activities in team meetings. We will explore how regular recognition sessions reinforce a positive atmosphere.

By incorporating recognition, leaders keep appreciation at the forefront.

Encouraging Peer-to-Peer Recognition

Leaders will encourage peer-to-peer recognition among team members. We will discuss the benefits of team members acknowledging each other's contributions.

By encouraging peer recognition, leaders strengthen team camaraderie.

Leading by Example

Leaders will lead by example by recognizing and appreciating their team's efforts. We will discuss how genuine appreciation from leaders inspires the team.

By leading by example, leaders set the tone for a culture of recognition.

Celebrating Task Completion

Leaders will celebrate successful task completion with the team. We will discuss the significance of acknowledging collective efforts and achievements.

By celebrating completion, leaders foster team spirit and camaraderie.

Celebrating task completion is a vital part of effective task delegation. In this chapter, we explore the significance of celebration, techniques for commemorating achievements, and the impact on team spirit and motivation.

Understanding the Importance of Celebration

Leaders will understand the critical importance of celebrating task completion. We will explore how celebrating achievements reinforces a sense of accomplishment and boosts team morale.

By valuing celebration, leaders nurture a culture of appreciation and recognition.

Organizing Completion Ceremonies

Leaders will organize completion ceremonies to honor successful task execution. We will discuss techniques for planning meaningful and memorable events.

By organizing ceremonies, leaders show appreciation for the team's hard work.

Commending Team Efforts

Leaders will commend the collective efforts of the team in completing tasks. We will explore how acknowledging teamwork fosters collaboration.

By commending team efforts, leaders strengthen team cohesion.

Recognizing Individual Contributions

Leaders will recognize individual contributions to task completion. We will discuss techniques for highlighting individual achievements.

By recognizing individuals, leaders inspire a sense of pride and personal growth.

Sharing Success Stories

Leaders will share success stories of completed tasks with the entire organization. We will explore how storytelling promotes a positive team image.

By sharing success stories, leaders showcase the team's impact on the organization.

Offering Tokens of Appreciation

Leaders will offer tokens of appreciation to team members for their efforts. We will discuss how small gestures can have a significant impact on team motivation.

By offering tokens of appreciation, leaders show gratitude for dedication.

Organizing Team Outings or Activities

Leaders will organize team outings or activities as a reward for successful task completion. We will explore how team bonding enhances collaboration.

By organizing outings, leaders strengthen team relationships.

Providing Opportunities for Feedback

Leaders will provide opportunities for team members to offer feedback on the task completion process. We will discuss how feedback supports continuous improvement.

By providing feedback opportunities, leaders demonstrate a commitment to growth.

Documenting Achievements

Leaders will document task achievements to commemorate successes. We will explore the benefits of keeping records of completed tasks.

By documenting achievements, leaders create a record of the team's accomplishments.

Creating a Wall of Fame

Leaders will create a "Wall of Fame" to showcase completed tasks and team member contributions. We will discuss how visual recognition reinforces a culture of excellence.

By creating a Wall of Fame, leaders celebrate the team's achievements.

Conclusion

The delegation process is a comprehensive approach to effective task distribution. In this chapter, leaders understand how to identify delegation opportunities, analyze task requirements, and select the right team members.

By communicating decisions, providing support, and monitoring progress, leaders facilitate successful task execution. Addressing challenges, offering feedback, and recognizing accomplishments contribute to a motivated and high-performing team.

Chapter 8: Overcoming Delegation Hurdles

Overcoming delegation hurdles is essential for successful task distribution. In this chapter, we explore common challenges in delegation, techniques for addressing obstacles, and the impact on leadership effectiveness and team performance.

Understanding Delegation Challenges

Leaders will understand the diverse challenges they may encounter in the delegation process. We will explore common hurdles and their potential impact on task execution.

By understanding challenges, leaders prepare for effective problem-solving.

Delegation is a powerful leadership tool, but it comes with its unique set of challenges. In this chapter, we delve into the various obstacles and complexities that leaders may encounter during the delegation process. By understanding these challenges, leaders can develop effective strategies to overcome them and ensure successful task execution.

Recognizing Fear of Letting Go

One of the primary challenges in delegation is the fear of letting go of control. Leaders may be hesitant to entrust important tasks to others, fearing potential mistakes or the loss of their sense of ownership.

Addressing Perfectionism and Micromanagement

Perfectionism and micromanagement tendencies can hinder delegation efforts. Leaders who strive for perfection may find it difficult to delegate tasks, as they fear that others may not meet their high standards.

Handling Time Constraints

Leaders often face time constraints that limit their ability to effectively delegate tasks. Time management becomes crucial to ensure that leaders allocate sufficient time for the delegation process while balancing other responsibilities.

Navigating Cultural and Organizational Barriers

In some organizational cultures, delegation may not be the norm, or there may be specific organizational barriers that hinder effective task distribution. Leaders must navigate these cultural and organizational factors to promote delegation as an essential aspect of leadership.

Managing Difficult Team Members

Delegating tasks to difficult team members can be challenging. Some team members may resist taking on additional responsibilities, or they may not perform adequately in delegated tasks.

Addressing Lack of Skills or Resources

Delegating tasks that require specific skills or resources can be problematic when team members lack the necessary capabilities. Leaders must address these limitations and provide appropriate training and resources to support successful task execution.

Building Trust and Confidence

Delegation relies heavily on trust and confidence between leaders and their team members. Building trust can be a challenge, especially when team members are inexperienced or new to their roles.

Overcoming Communication Barriers

Effective communication is crucial for successful delegation. Communication barriers, such as language differences or poor communication channels, can impede task understanding and performance.

Adapting Delegation Approaches

Leaders must be adaptable in their delegation approaches to suit individual team members' needs and abilities. One approach may not fit all team members, and leaders need to tailor their delegation style accordingly.

Identifying Personal Resistance to Delegation

Leaders will identify personal resistance to delegation. We will discuss techniques for overcoming the fear of losing control and trusting team members.

By addressing personal resistance, leaders embrace the power of delegation.

Personal resistance to delegation is a common challenge faced by many leaders. In this chapter, we delve into the reasons behind this resistance, explore its impact on leadership effectiveness, and discuss techniques for overcoming these barriers.

Understanding the Fear of Losing Control

One significant reason for personal resistance to delegation is the fear of losing control. Leaders may be reluctant to delegate tasks because they worry that they won't have complete control over the outcome or that the task won't be performed up to their standards.

Recognizing Perceived Inadequacy

Leaders may resist delegation because they perceive themselves as the only ones capable of handling certain tasks. They may doubt their team members' abilities, believing that they are the most skilled or knowledgeable individuals to get the job done.

Experiencing a Sense of Ownership

Another challenge is the sense of ownership leaders feel over their responsibilities. They may find it challenging to let go of tasks they have been handling for a long time, as they are deeply invested in the outcomes and have a sense of pride in their work.

Fear of Negative Outcomes

Leaders may fear negative outcomes if they delegate tasks. They worry that mistakes or failures will reflect poorly on them as leaders and may harm their reputation.

Perfectionism and Trust Issues

Perfectionism can also play a role in resistance to delegation. Leaders who strive for perfection may believe that they are the only ones who can achieve the desired results. Additionally, trust issues with team members can make it difficult for leaders to delegate tasks confidently.

Lack of Time for Training and Oversight

Leaders may resist delegation because they feel they don't have the time to train team members adequately or provide sufficient oversight during task execution.

Feeling Indispensable

Leaders may resist delegation because they fear becoming dispensable or believe that their value lies in being the sole expert in certain areas.

Overcoming Personal Resistance

Overcoming personal resistance to delegation is crucial for effective leadership. In this chapter, we will discuss techniques for addressing these challenges, such as:

1. Recognizing the benefits of delegation for personal and team growth.

2. Identifying tasks suitable for delegation and starting with small, less critical tasks.

3. Providing training and support to build team members' skills and confidence.

4. Establishing clear communication channels and expectations.

5. Acknowledging team members' achievements and successes in delegated tasks.

6. Emphasizing the importance of teamwork and collaboration.

Handling Perfectionism and Micromanagement Tendencies

Leaders will handle perfectionism and micromanagement tendencies that hinder delegation. We will explore techniques for letting go of excessive control.

By overcoming micromanagement, leaders empower their team to excel.

Perfectionism and micromanagement tendencies can significantly hinder effective delegation. In this chapter, we explore the impact of these traits on leadership and team dynamics and discuss techniques for overcoming these challenges.

Understanding Perfectionism and Micromanagement

Perfectionism is the desire to achieve flawless results, while micromanagement involves excessive control and oversight of delegated tasks. Both traits can arise from a leader's desire for excellence but may lead to counterproductive outcomes.

Recognizing the Negative Impact

Perfectionism and micromanagement can have adverse effects on team morale and productivity. Team members may feel undervalued, disempowered, and lose motivation when their contributions are constantly scrutinized.

Embracing the Power of Delegation

Leaders must recognize that delegation empowers team members and fosters professional growth. Embracing delegation as a leadership approach can help shift the focus from perfectionism and micromanagement to collaborative teamwork.

Setting Realistic Expectations

Leaders need to set realistic expectations for task outcomes. Understanding that perfection is often unattainable and that mistakes are a part of the learning process can reduce the pressure to achieve flawless results.

Providing Clear Guidelines and Support

Clear guidelines and instructions at the outset of task delegation can alleviate the need for excessive oversight. Additionally, providing ongoing support and feedback ensures that team members feel confident and guided throughout the task.

Learning to Trust Team Members

Building trust in team members' abilities is crucial for overcoming micromanagement tendencies. Leaders must recognize that their team members are capable and allow them the autonomy to make decisions.

Encouraging a Culture of Learning

Creating a culture that values learning and growth over perfection can mitigate the negative impact of perfectionism. Leaders can encourage experimentation, innovation, and learning from mistakes.

Practicing Delegation in Gradual Steps

Leaders who struggle with delegation can start with gradual steps. Delegating smaller, less critical tasks initially can help build confidence and experience in delegation.

Seeking Feedback and Self-Reflection

Leaders should seek feedback from team members about their delegation approach and be open to self-reflection. Understanding how their actions affect the team can help them modify their behavior.

Focusing on the Big Picture

Leaders should focus on the big picture and overall team goals rather than getting lost in the details. This perspective helps keep the team aligned and motivated.

Dealing with Time Constraints

Leaders will address time constraints that may limit their ability to delegate effectively. We will discuss time management techniques to allocate sufficient time for delegation.

By managing time effectively, leaders prioritize delegation as a leadership priority.

Time constraints can be a significant challenge for leaders when it comes to effective delegation. In this chapter, we explore the impact of time limitations on delegation efforts and discuss strategies to manage time effectively while ensuring successful task distribution.

Understanding the Value of Delegation

Leaders must recognize the value of delegation in optimizing their time and enhancing team productivity. Delegation allows leaders to focus on strategic tasks and long-term goals while empowering their team to handle day-to-day responsibilities.

Prioritizing Delegation as a Leadership Priority

Delegation should be prioritized as a core leadership responsibility. By recognizing its importance, leaders can allocate dedicated time for planning, communication, and monitoring of delegated tasks.

Identifying Suitable Tasks for Delegation

Leaders should identify tasks that are suitable for delegation, considering factors such as complexity, urgency, and team members' skills. By delegating appropriate tasks, leaders can streamline their workload.

Streamlining the Delegation Process

To save time in the delegation process, leaders can develop streamlined procedures and templates for task assignment, instructions, and reporting. This approach ensures consistency and efficiency.

Empowering Team Members to Make Decisions

By empowering team members to make decisions within predefined boundaries, leaders reduce the need for constant consultation and approval. Trusting team members' judgment saves time and fosters autonomy.

Setting Clear Expectations and Deadlines

Clear and concise communication regarding task expectations and deadlines helps minimize follow-up and clarification requests. Team members can work efficiently when they understand their responsibilities.

Utilizing Technology and Tools

Leaders can leverage technology and task management tools to streamline delegation and monitor progress. Project management software, communication platforms, and scheduling tools can enhance efficiency.

Avoiding Micro-Management

Leaders should avoid micro-management tendencies, as it consumes time and undermines team members' confidence. Trusting the team's capabilities promotes a more efficient workflow.

Delegating to Develop Skills and Efficiency

Delegating tasks that allow team members to develop their skills and expertise fosters long-term efficiency. As team members become more proficient, they require less oversight, saving leaders time.

Seeking Assistance When Needed

Leaders should not hesitate to seek assistance from colleagues or superiors when faced with time constraints. Collaboration and delegation to peers can help distribute the workload effectively.

Leaders will navigate cultural and organizational barriers that may impede delegation efforts. We will explore techniques for fostering a delegation-friendly culture.

By navigating barriers, leaders create an environment conducive to delegation.

Cultural and organizational barriers can present significant challenges in the delegation process. In this chapter, we explore the impact of these barriers on delegation efforts and discuss techniques for navigating them to foster a delegation-friendly environment.

Understanding Cultural and Organizational Influences

Cultural and organizational factors shape the beliefs, norms, and practices within a team or company. These influences can impact the perception and acceptance of delegation as a leadership practice.

Recognizing Cultural Differences

Leaders must be aware of cultural differences within their team or organization that may affect attitudes towards delegation. Some cultures may value individual responsibility over team collaboration, impacting how tasks are assigned and managed.

Promoting a Delegation-Friendly Culture

To navigate cultural barriers, leaders should actively promote a delegation-friendly culture. They can do so by emphasizing the benefits of delegation, providing training, and celebrating successful examples of delegation.

Identifying Organizational Resistance

Organizational structures and hierarchies can create resistance to delegation. Leaders must identify barriers such as a top-down decision-making approach that discourages delegation.

Engaging with Organizational Leaders

Leaders should engage with higher-level organizational leaders to gain support for delegation efforts. Demonstrating the positive impact of delegation on team performance can garner organizational backing.

Addressing Fear of Failure

Organizational cultures that stigmatize failure may discourage delegation. Leaders should create an environment where taking calculated risks and learning from mistakes are encouraged.

Building Trust with Team Members

Building trust is essential in overcoming cultural and organizational barriers. Leaders should establish open communication channels, listen to team members' concerns, and address them promptly.

Customizing Delegation Approaches

Customizing delegation approaches to fit the organization's unique needs and culture can increase receptiveness. Leaders should be adaptable and considerate of the existing dynamics.

Communicating Clearly and Effectively

Clear and effective communication is crucial when navigating barriers. Leaders should communicate task expectations, responsibilities, and outcomes explicitly to avoid misunderstandings.

Leading by Example

Leaders must lead by example and demonstrate effective delegation practices. When team members see leaders effectively delegating and supporting their efforts, they are more likely to embrace delegation.

Managing Difficult Team Members

Leaders will manage difficult team members who resist or underperform in delegated tasks. We will discuss techniques for addressing challenges and fostering improvement.

By managing difficult team members, leaders promote accountability.

Managing difficult team members is a critical aspect of effective delegation. In this chapter, we explore strategies for handling challenging individuals to ensure successful task delegation and maintain a harmonious team dynamic.

Recognizing Difficult Team Member Behaviors

Leaders must be able to recognize difficult behaviors in team members. These may include resistance to taking on delegated tasks, lack of motivation, or disruptive attitudes.

Addressing the Root Cause of Difficulties

Understanding the root cause of difficult behaviors is essential. Leaders should have open conversations with team members to identify underlying issues and concerns.

Providing Clarity and Direction

Clear and specific task instructions help alleviate confusion and uncertainty for difficult team members. Providing a sense of direction can improve their engagement in the delegated tasks.

Offering Support and Resources

Difficult team members may struggle with delegated tasks due to inadequate skills or resources. Leaders should provide necessary support, training, and resources to facilitate their success.

Setting Boundaries and Expectations

Establishing clear boundaries and expectations is crucial when dealing with disruptive behavior. Leaders should communicate the team's code of conduct and address any violations promptly.

Using Positive Reinforcement

Positive reinforcement can be an effective way to encourage difficult team members. Recognizing their efforts and progress can boost motivation and foster a positive attitude towards delegation.

Coaching and Mentorship

Coaching and mentorship can help difficult team members improve their performance. Leaders should offer guidance and constructive feedback to support their growth.

Handling Underperformance

If difficult team members consistently underperform, leaders may need to address the issue directly. Performance improvement plans and progressive disciplinary actions can be necessary in such cases.

Encouraging Peer Support

Encouraging peer support and collaboration can help integrate difficult team members into the delegation process. Positive team dynamics can influence their behavior positively.

In cases of severe conflicts, leaders may seek mediation from HR or higher management to resolve interpersonal issues and restore team harmony.

Addressing Lack of Skills or Resources

Leaders will address the lack of skills or resources required for certain tasks. We will explore how training and resource allocation can bridge gaps.

By addressing limitations, leaders optimize task allocation.

Addressing the lack of skills or resources is a critical aspect of effective delegation. In this chapter, we explore strategies for overcoming these challenges to ensure successful task distribution and empower team members.

Assessing Team Members' Skills and Abilities

Leaders must assess the skills and abilities of their team members to identify areas where additional support may be needed. This assessment helps in making informed decisions about task delegation.

Providing Training and Development Opportunities

If team members lack certain skills required for delegated tasks, leaders should provide appropriate training and development opportunities. Training sessions, workshops, and mentorship can enhance their capabilities.

Encouraging Skill-Sharing Among Team Members

Encouraging skill-sharing among team members fosters a collaborative environment where team members learn from each other's expertise. Peer-to-peer knowledge transfer can bridge skill gaps.

Seeking External Resources or Expertise

When internal resources are insufficient, leaders can seek external resources or expertise. This may include outsourcing certain tasks or collaborating with external specialists.

Breaking Down Complex Tasks

Breaking down complex tasks into smaller, manageable components can make delegation more feasible for team members with limited resources. This approach promotes task success and gradual skill development.

Offering Support and Guidance

Leaders should offer ongoing support and guidance to team members, especially when they are dealing with resource constraints. Being available for questions and providing assistance can boost their confidence.

Empowering Team Members to Find Solutions

Encouraging team members to find creative solutions to resource limitations empowers them to take ownership of the delegation process. Leaders should foster a problem-solving mindset.

Setting Realistic Expectations

Leaders must set realistic expectations for delegated tasks, considering the available resources. Unrealistic expectations can lead to frustration and disengagement among team members.

Monitoring Resource Allocation

Effective resource allocation is vital for successful delegation. Leaders should ensure that team members have the necessary tools, equipment, and support to complete their tasks.

Documenting Resource Needs and Constraints

Documenting resource needs and constraints helps leaders plan and allocate resources more effectively in future delegation efforts.

Building Trust and Confidence

Leaders will build trust and confidence in their team's abilities. We will discuss techniques for communicating expectations and setting team members up for success.

By building trust, leaders inspire task ownership and dedication.

Building trust and confidence is fundamental to effective delegation. In this chapter, we explore the significance of trust in delegation, discuss techniques for fostering trust, and examine its impact on team performance and success.

Understanding the Role of Trust in Delegation

Trust is the foundation of successful delegation. Team members must trust their leaders' judgment and intentions, while leaders must have confidence in their team members' capabilities.

Leading by Example

Leaders should lead by example and demonstrate trust in their team members. Being transparent, reliable, and accountable sets the tone for a trusting relationship.

Communicating Openly and Transparently

Open and transparent communication builds trust between leaders and team members. Leaders should share information, goals, and challenges openly.

Empowering Team Members

Empowering team members to make decisions and take ownership of tasks instills confidence and trust in their abilities. Leaders should avoid micromanaging and encourage autonomy.

Providing Clear Expectations

Clear and explicit expectations set the groundwork for trust. When team members understand what is expected of them, they can confidently execute their tasks.

Encouraging Risk-Taking and Learning from Mistakes

Leaders should encourage calculated risk-taking and view mistakes as opportunities for learning. This approach fosters an environment where team members feel safe to take initiative.

Acknowledging and Valuing Contributions

Recognizing and valuing team members' contributions reinforces their sense of worth and trust in the delegation process. Leaders should celebrate successes and acknowledge efforts.

Being Supportive and Approachable

Leaders should be approachable and supportive of team members. Listening to their concerns and providing assistance when needed fosters a trusting relationship.

Being Available for Guidance

Being available for guidance and support shows team members that leaders are invested in their success. Leaders should make time for one-on-one discussions when team members require assistance.

Avoiding Blame and Fostering Accountability

Leaders should avoid blaming team members for mistakes and instead promote a culture of accountability. Addressing issues constructively encourages growth and trust.

Building Personal Connections

Building personal connections with team members goes a long way in building trust. Leaders should take an interest in their team members' well-being and professional growth.

Overcoming Communication Barriers

Leaders will overcome communication barriers that hinder effective delegation. We will explore how improving communication channels enhances task understanding.

By overcoming barriers, leaders ensure clarity and alignment.

Effective communication is essential for successful delegation. In this chapter, we explore the common communication barriers that hinder delegation efforts and discuss strategies for overcoming these challenges to ensure clear and efficient task distribution.

Recognizing Common Communication Barriers

Leaders must be aware of the common communication barriers that can impact the delegation process. These barriers may include language differences, misinterpretations, distractions, and information overload.

Improving Clarity and Precision

Clear and precise communication is critical for successful delegation. Leaders should use simple language, avoid jargon, and provide specific instructions to minimize misunderstandings.

Active Listening and Feedback

Active listening and seeking feedback from team members promote a two-way communication flow. Leaders should encourage open discussions to ensure that messages are accurately received and understood.

Using Multiple Communication Channels

Using various communication channels, such as email, in-person meetings, and video calls, ensures that messages reach team members effectively. Different team members may prefer different communication methods.

Addressing Language and Cultural Differences

Language and cultural differences can create communication challenges, especially in diverse teams. Leaders should be sensitive to these differences and make an effort to bridge any gaps.

Reducing Noise and Distractions

Minimizing noise and distractions during communication helps maintain focus and clarity. Leaders should choose suitable environments for discussions and ensure that team members can concentrate.

Encouraging Open and Honest Communication

Leaders should foster an environment where team members feel comfortable expressing their thoughts and concerns openly. Encouraging honest communication builds trust and improves delegation outcomes.

Using Visual Aids and Documentation

Visual aids and written documentation can enhance understanding, especially for complex tasks. Leaders can use diagrams, charts, and written instructions to complement verbal communication.

Confirming Understanding

Leaders should confirm that team members have understood their instructions and expectations. Requesting team members to summarize or repeat instructions helps avoid miscommunication.

Regular Check-ins and Updates

Regular check-ins and updates on task progress promote ongoing communication. Leaders can provide feedback, address concerns, and make adjustments if needed.

Adapting Delegation Approaches

Leaders will adapt their delegation approaches to suit individual team members' needs. We will discuss how flexible leadership promotes team engagement.

By adapting approaches, leaders maximize team potential.

Adaptability is crucial for effective delegation. In this chapter, we explore the significance of adapting delegation approaches to suit different team members' needs and abilities. We also discuss the impact of flexible leadership on team engagement and performance.

Recognizing Individual Differences

Each team member is unique, with varying skills, preferences, and strengths. Leaders must recognize these individual differences and adapt their delegation approach accordingly.

Understanding Different Learning Styles

Different team members may have different learning styles, such as visual, auditory, or kinesthetic. Leaders should consider these preferences when providing instructions and training.

Tailoring Communication Methods

Adapting communication methods to suit individual team members' preferences enhances understanding. Some team members may prefer face-to-face communication, while others may prefer written instructions.

Providing Different Levels of Support

Some team members may require more support and guidance during the delegation process. Leaders should be prepared to offer additional assistance to those who need it.

Encouraging Autonomy for Experienced Members

Experienced team members may thrive with greater autonomy. Leaders should provide them with more independence in task execution to promote engagement and motivation.

Building Skills for Less Experienced Members

For less experienced team members, leaders should focus on building skills through training and mentorship. Gradual delegation of more complex tasks can foster their development.

Flexibility in Task Allocation

Being flexible in task allocation allows leaders to match tasks with team members' interests and abilities. This approach promotes a sense of ownership and dedication to the delegated tasks.

Adjusting Delegation Levels

Leaders should adjust the level of delegation based on team members' growth and capabilities. Gradually increasing responsibility as team members become more proficient enhances their self-confidence.

Adapting to Changing Situations

Leaders should be adaptable to changing situations, such as project demands or team dynamics. Adjusting delegation approaches when circumstances evolve ensures effectiveness.

Promoting Continuous Feedback

Continuous feedback from team members helps leaders understand what approaches work best for each individual. This feedback enables leaders to refine their delegation techniques.

Conclusion

Overcoming delegation hurdles is integral to effective task distribution. In this chapter, leaders understand delegation challenges, identify personal resistance, and address micromanagement tendencies.

By navigating time constraints, managing difficult team members, and building trust, leaders optimize delegation outcomes. Overcoming barriers, adapting approaches, and enhancing communication foster a dynamic and high-performing team.

Chapter 9: Empowering Through Delegation

Empowering team members through delegation is the key to unlocking their full potential and achieving remarkable results. In this chapter, we explore the transformative power of delegation in fostering a culture of empowerment and driving individual and team growth.

Understanding the Impact of Empowerment

Empowerment enables team members to take ownership of their tasks, make decisions, and contribute meaningfully to the organization's goals. It boosts morale, motivation, and overall job satisfaction.

Empowerment is a potent force that drives positive outcomes for both individuals and organizations. In this chapter, we delve into the profound impact of empowerment on team members, leaders, and the overall success of the delegation process.

Enhancing Job Satisfaction and Engagement

Empowered team members experience higher job satisfaction as they feel valued and trusted. This sense of ownership leads to increased engagement and commitment to their roles.

Boosting Motivation and Productivity

Empowerment fuels intrinsic motivation, encouraging team members to take initiative and excel in their tasks. When individuals feel empowered, their productivity and performance levels rise significantly.

Fostering Innovation and Creativity

Empowered team members are more likely to think creatively and contribute innovative ideas. A culture of empowerment encourages experimentation and risk-taking, fostering a spirit of innovation.

Developing Confidence and Self-Efficacy

Delegation empowers team members by offering them opportunities to develop new skills and take on challenges. As individuals successfully complete delegated tasks, their confidence and self-efficacy grow.

Creating a Positive Work Environment

A work environment built on empowerment fosters positivity and trust. When team members feel empowered, they are more likely to collaborate, support each other, and celebrate collective success.

Improving Decision-Making and Problem-Solving

Empowered team members are entrusted with decision-making authority, enabling quicker and more efficient problem-solving. This reduces the burden on leaders and promotes agility.

Unlocking Leadership Potential

Delegation allows emerging leaders to demonstrate their potential and abilities. Identifying and empowering future leaders through delegation cultivates a pipeline of skilled and capable leaders.

Driving Employee Retention and Loyalty

Empowerment plays a significant role in employee retention. Team members who feel empowered are more likely to remain committed and loyal to the organization.

Enhancing Adaptability and Resilience

Empowered team members are better equipped to handle change and uncertainty. Their adaptability and resilience enable them to navigate challenges and opportunities effectively.

Aligning Team Goals with Organizational Objectives

Empowerment aligns team goals with organizational objectives. When team members have autonomy and accountability, they work toward shared success.

Creating a Culture of Empowerment

Leaders play a vital role in creating a culture of empowerment. By delegating responsibilities and encouraging autonomy, leaders empower their team members to excel.

Building a culture of empowerment is a fundamental aspect of effective delegation. In this chapter, we explore the steps leaders can take to foster an environment where empowerment thrives, enabling team members to reach their full potential.

Setting Clear Expectations

Clear expectations form the foundation of empowerment. Leaders should communicate organizational goals, individual responsibilities, and performance metrics to align team efforts.

Encouraging Open Communication

Open communication channels promote transparency and trust. Leaders should actively listen to team members' ideas, concerns, and feedback, fostering a culture of collaboration.

Providing Autonomy and Decision-Making Authority

Empowerment is about granting team members the autonomy to make decisions related to their delegated tasks. Leaders should provide the necessary authority and guidance.

Recognizing and Celebrating Achievements

Acknowledging team members' accomplishments reinforces their sense of empowerment. Regular recognition and celebration of successes inspire continued dedication.

Promoting Learning and Growth

A culture of empowerment supports continuous learning and growth. Leaders should encourage skill development and offer opportunities for professional advancement.

Embracing a Fail-Forward Mentality

Empowerment involves accepting that failures are part of the learning process. Leaders should embrace a fail-forward mentality, encouraging team members to learn from mistakes.

Supporting Risk-Taking and Experimentation

Empowerment thrives when team members feel encouraged to take calculated risks and experiment with new ideas. Leaders should foster a safe environment for innovation.

Offering Mentorship and Coaching

Mentorship and coaching demonstrate a commitment to team members' development. Leaders should provide guidance and support to nurture their skills.

Building Trust through Consistency

Consistency in delegation practices builds trust. Team members must trust that leaders will consistently empower them and recognize their contributions.

Encouraging Collaboration and Teamwork

Empowerment extends beyond individual efforts. Leaders should foster collaboration and teamwork, where collective achievements are celebrated.

Delegation as a Development Tool

Delegation serves as a powerful development tool for team members. It allows them to build new skills, gain experience, and grow professionally.

Delegation serves as a powerful tool for individual and team development. In this chapter, we delve into the transformative role of delegation in fostering professional growth and building a skilled and resilient workforce.

Identifying Individual Strengths and Growth Areas

Delegation allows leaders to identify team members' strengths and areas for development. Understanding these attributes helps leaders tailor tasks to match individual capabilities.

Providing Learning Opportunities

Delegating new and challenging tasks provides team members with valuable learning opportunities. Exposure to diverse tasks broadens their skill set and enhances their versatility.

Building Skills and Expertise

Delegation is an avenue for team members to build specialized skills and expertise. By handling diverse responsibilities, team members become subject matter experts in their respective areas.

Promoting Leadership Development

Delegating leadership responsibilities empowers emerging leaders to grow and develop their managerial capabilities. As leaders nurture future leaders, they create a leadership pipeline within the organization.

Boosting Confidence and Initiative

Successful completion of delegated tasks boosts team members' confidence and initiative. Empowered individuals are more likely to take on additional responsibilities willingly.

Cultivating Problem-Solving and Decision-Making Skills

Delegation fosters critical problem-solving and decision-making skills. Team members must make informed choices and handle challenges independently.

Encouraging Accountability and Responsibility

Delegation instills a sense of accountability and responsibility in team members. Knowing that they are trusted to deliver results motivates them to take ownership of their work.

Facilitating Adaptability and Resilience

As team members tackle various tasks, they develop adaptability and resilience in the face of change and uncertainty. These skills are vital for navigating dynamic work environments.

Creating a Learning Organization

Delegation supports the development of a learning organization, where continuous learning and improvement are ingrained in the organizational culture.

Nurturing a Culture of Mentoring and Collaboration

Delegation promotes a culture of mentoring, where experienced team members guide and support their colleagues. Collaboration and knowledge sharing become integral to team success.

Encouraging Creativity and Innovation

Empowered team members are more likely to think creatively and propose innovative solutions. Delegation encourages them to explore new ideas and take calculated risks.

Encouraging creativity and innovation is a powerful outcome of effective delegation. In this chapter, we explore how delegation can become a catalyst for unleashing team members' creative potential and driving forward-thinking solutions.

Recognizing the Value of Creativity and Innovation

Leaders must recognize the importance of creativity and innovation in driving organizational growth and competitiveness. Delegation plays a key role in fostering a culture that embraces new ideas.

Creating an Environment of Psychological Safety

Psychological safety is essential for encouraging creativity. Leaders should create an environment where team members feel safe to express unique perspectives and experiment without fear of judgment.

Delegating Projects with Room for Creativity

Delegating projects that allow for creative input provides team members with opportunities to innovate. Leaders should provide a degree of autonomy for creativity to flourish.

Encouraging Diverse Perspectives

Delegation facilitates collaboration among team members with diverse perspectives and expertise. Encouraging open discussions allows for the cross-pollination of ideas.

Rewarding and Recognizing Creative Contributions

Recognizing and rewarding creative contributions incentivizes innovation. Leaders should celebrate successful creative endeavors to motivate continued creativity.

Supporting Risk-Taking and Learning from Failures

Delegation encourages calculated risk-taking. Leaders should embrace failure as a stepping stone to innovation and foster a learning culture that embraces valuable lessons from setbacks.

Promoting Brainstorming and Idea Generation

Delegation can include brainstorming sessions to generate innovative ideas. Leaders should actively encourage idea sharing and create platforms for ideation.

Providing Resources for Experimentation

Delegation should involve providing resources and support for experimentation. Leaders should allocate time, budget, and tools to test new ideas.

Leveraging Technology and Innovation Tools

Leaders should leverage technology and innovation tools to enhance the creative process. Collaboration platforms and idea management software can streamline innovation efforts.

Leading by Example with Creativity

Leaders should demonstrate creativity in their own approaches to problem-solving and decision-making. Leading by example inspires creativity throughout the team.

Fostering Leadership Potential

Delegation provides opportunities for team members to showcase their leadership potential. Leaders should identify emerging leaders and delegate tasks that align with their strengths.

Delegation is a powerful tool for nurturing and fostering leadership potential within a team. In this chapter, we explore how effective delegation can identify emerging leaders, develop their skills, and build a pipeline of future leaders.

Recognizing Emerging Leaders

Delegation allows leaders to identify team members who exhibit leadership qualities and potential. Observing how individuals handle responsibility and decision-making sheds light on their leadership capabilities.

Delegating Challenging Tasks and Projects

Assigning challenging tasks and projects to emerging leaders provides them with opportunities to showcase their leadership skills. Leaders should provide the necessary support and guidance.

Offering Leadership Development Opportunities

Leadership development programs and workshops provide emerging leaders with the knowledge and skills they need to excel. Delegation should be combined with ongoing learning initiatives.

Mentoring and Coaching

Mentoring and coaching are essential in nurturing leadership potential. Leaders should take on a mentoring role, providing guidance and feedback to help emerging leaders grow.

Encouraging Initiative and Decision-Making

Delegation encourages emerging leaders to take initiative and make decisions independently. Leaders should empower them to be proactive and accountable for their actions.

Promoting Team Leadership

Delegating leadership responsibilities within teams fosters a collaborative leadership approach. Shared leadership encourages collective problem-solving and decision-making.

Providing Exposure to Senior Leadership

Exposing emerging leaders to senior leadership and high-level decision-making offers valuable insights and experiences. Leaders should provide opportunities for interactions with top executives.

Creating a Culture of Leadership Development

Fostering a culture of leadership development encourages all team members to aspire to leadership roles. Delegation should be an integral part of this growth-oriented culture.

Building Leadership Competencies

Delegation can be tailored to develop specific leadership competencies, such as communication, conflict resolution, and strategic thinking.

Succession Planning

Delegation supports succession planning efforts. Identifying and nurturing emerging leaders ensures a smooth transition when leadership positions become vacant.

Developing Trust and Collaboration

Empowerment fosters trust between leaders and team members, as well as among team members themselves. A trusting environment enhances collaboration and teamwork.

Trust and collaboration are vital for effective delegation and team success. In this chapter, we explore how leaders can develop trust among team members and foster a collaborative environment that enhances delegation outcomes.

Building Trust through Transparent Communication

Transparent communication is the foundation of trust. Leaders should be honest, open, and consistent in their communication with team members.

Leading by Example with Trustworthiness

Leaders should demonstrate trustworthiness in their actions and decisions. Being reliable and accountable sets a positive example for team members.

Empowering Team Members with Autonomy

Delegating authority and providing team members with autonomy builds trust. Empowered team members feel valued and trusted to make decisions.

Encouraging Collaboration over Competition

Promoting a collaborative, rather than a competitive, environment fosters trust among team members. Collaboration encourages knowledge sharing and mutual support.

Creating Opportunities for Team-Building

Team-building activities and workshops strengthen relationships among team members. Leaders should organize team-building exercises to enhance collaboration.

Resolving Conflicts Constructively

Conflict is inevitable in any team. Leaders should address conflicts constructively, promoting open communication and finding win-win solutions.

Seeking Input and Feedback

Leaders should actively seek input and feedback from team members. Valuing their opinions enhances trust and collaboration.

Recognizing and Celebrating Collective Success

Recognizing and celebrating collective successes reinforces collaboration. Acknowledging team achievements fosters a sense of camaraderie.

Encouraging Interdisciplinary Collaboration

Delegation can involve cross-functional collaboration. Leaders should encourage team members from different departments to work together on projects.

Promoting Inclusivity and Diversity

Inclusivity and diversity enrich team dynamics. Leaders should embrace diversity and create an inclusive environment where everyone's contributions are valued.

Delegating Authority, Not Just Tasks

Leaders should delegate authority, not just tasks. Empowered team members are given decision-making power, enabling them to take action without constant approval.

Delegating authority goes beyond assigning tasks; it involves empowering team members to make decisions and take ownership of their work. In this chapter, we explore the significance of delegating authority and the transformative impact it can have on team performance and individual growth.

Understanding the Difference Between Task Delegation and Authority Delegation

Task delegation involves assigning specific responsibilities, while authority delegation grants team members decision-making power. Leaders should combine both to empower their team fully.

Empowering Team Members with Decision-Making Authority

Delegating decision-making authority empowers team members to act independently and take initiative. Leaders should trust their team to make informed choices.

Providing Guidelines and Boundaries

While granting authority, leaders should set clear guidelines and boundaries to ensure decisions align with organizational goals and values.

Encouraging Risk-Taking and Innovation

Delegating authority encourages calculated risk-taking and promotes innovative thinking. Team members are more likely to explore new ideas when they have the freedom to make decisions.

Recognizing the Impact of Empowerment

Empowering team members with authority fosters a sense of ownership and accountability. This sense of ownership motivates them to excel in their roles.

Supporting Team Members in Decision-Making

Leaders should offer support and guidance to team members when they face challenging decisions. A supportive environment encourages growth and development.

Building Trust through Authority Delegation

Delegating authority builds trust between leaders and team members. Trust is essential for creating a positive and productive work culture.

Ensuring Accountability in Decision-Making

With authority comes responsibility. Leaders should ensure team members are accountable for their decisions and their impact on the team and organization.

Recognizing and Celebrating Successful Decisions

Acknowledging successful decisions and outcomes reinforces the value of authority delegation. Celebrating accomplishments boosts team morale.

Empowering Emerging Leaders through Authority Delegation

Authority delegation is a potent tool for nurturing emerging leaders. Leaders should delegate authority to those with leadership potential to foster their growth.

Empowerment in Challenging Times

In challenging times, delegation becomes even more critical in empowering team members. During crises or high-pressure situations, delegation can distribute responsibilities and improve problem-solving.

Empowerment becomes even more critical during challenging times when teams face uncertainty and adversity. In this chapter, we explore how delegation and empowerment can be powerful tools for navigating difficult situations and fostering resilience.

Understanding the Importance of Empowerment in Challenges

Challenging times require adaptive and resilient teams. Empowerment provides team members with the confidence and autonomy needed to overcome obstacles.

Communicating with Transparency and Compassion

Transparent and compassionate communication is crucial during difficult situations. Leaders should share information openly and empathetically to build trust.

Delegating Decision-Making for Rapid Response

During crises, quick decision-making is essential. Leaders should delegate decision-making authority to enable rapid responses to emerging challenges.

Supporting Team Members' Well-Being

Empowerment includes supporting team members' well-being during challenging times. Leaders should show empathy and provide resources for stress management.

Encouraging Problem-Solving and Innovation

Empowered teams are more likely to find innovative solutions to complex problems. Leaders should encourage creative problem-solving and experimentation.

Maintaining Focus on Goals and Priorities

Empowerment helps teams stay focused on essential goals and priorities. Leaders should align delegation with organizational objectives to maintain productivity.

Promoting Collaboration and Team Support

Empowered teams collaborate and support each other during challenging times. Leaders should foster a culture of teamwork and mutual assistance.

Recognizing and Celebrating Resilience

Recognizing team resilience and perseverance reinforces empowerment. Celebrating resilience encourages teams to stay strong during adversity.

Learning from Challenges and Failures

Challenging times offer valuable learning opportunities. Leaders should encourage teams to reflect on challenges and use failures as stepping stones to improvement.

Providing Opportunities for Skill Development

Empowerment includes providing opportunities for skill development even during difficult times. Leaders should offer training to enhance team capabilities.

Celebrating Success and Learning from Failure

Acknowledging successes and learning from failures are essential aspects of empowerment. Leaders should celebrate achievements and view mistakes as learning opportunities.

Celebrating success and learning from failure are essential aspects of an empowered team. In this chapter, we explore how leaders can foster a culture that values both success and failure as opportunities for growth and development.

Recognizing and Celebrating Team Achievements

Celebrating team successes reinforces a sense of accomplishment and motivates team members to strive for excellence. Leaders should acknowledge and appreciate collective achievements.

Individual Recognition for Contributions

Recognizing individual contributions within the team fosters a culture of appreciation. Leaders should celebrate each team member's unique efforts and value their role in the success.

Promoting a Growth Mindset

A growth mindset sees failure as an opportunity for learning and improvement. Leaders should encourage team members to embrace challenges and view setbacks as stepping stones to success.

Conducting Productive Post-Mortems

Post-mortems after both successful and failed projects are valuable for learning. Leaders should facilitate constructive discussions to identify areas for improvement.

Creating a Safe Environment for Learning

Leaders should create a safe space where team members feel comfortable sharing their experiences, including failures. A non-judgmental environment encourages openness.

Encouraging Knowledge Sharing

Knowledge sharing among team members allows lessons learned from both successes and failures to be disseminated. Leaders should encourage the exchange of insights.

Using Failure as a Learning Opportunity

Failure is an opportunity to learn, adapt, and innovate. Leaders should encourage experimentation and risk-taking while providing support when things don't go as planned.

Applying Lessons Learned to Future Projects

Learning from both success and failure should be applied to future projects. Leaders should use insights gained to improve processes and enhance team performance.

Balancing Accountability and Psychological Safety

Leaders should balance holding team members accountable for results with fostering psychological safety. A safe environment encourages risk-taking without fear of blame.

Continuous Improvement as a Team Norm

Continuous improvement should be ingrained in the team's culture. Leaders should promote an attitude of always seeking better ways to achieve goals.

Sustaining Empowerment Long-Term

Empowerment should be sustained as an ongoing practice. Leaders must consistently delegate and encourage team members to take initiative.

Sustaining empowerment as a long-term practice is crucial for fostering a high-performing and engaged team. In this chapter, we explore how leaders can continuously cultivate empowerment to ensure lasting success.

Making Empowerment a Core Leadership Principle

Empowerment should be a fundamental principle in leadership philosophy. Leaders should consistently prioritize delegation and autonomy in their approach.

Consistently Delegating Responsibilities

Leaders should delegate responsibilities on an ongoing basis, ensuring that team members have opportunities to take on new challenges regularly.

Encouraging a Learning and Development Culture

Promoting a culture of continuous learning and development reinforces empowerment. Leaders should provide resources and support for skill enhancement.

Recognizing and Rewarding Empowered Behavior

Recognizing and rewarding empowered behavior reinforces its value. Leaders should acknowledge team members who demonstrate initiative and accountability.

Providing Growth Opportunities

Empowerment goes hand in hand with growth opportunities. Leaders should create a roadmap for team members' professional development.

Fostering a Supportive Environment

A supportive environment encourages empowerment. Leaders should foster open communication and provide guidance when needed.

Emphasizing Collaboration and Teamwork

Empowerment should promote collaboration and teamwork. Leaders should celebrate collective achievements and encourage cooperation.

Seeking Feedback and Encouraging Continuous Improvement

Leaders should seek feedback from team members and use it to improve their delegation practices. Continuous improvement benefits both leaders and team members.

Empowering Emerging Leaders

Empowerment should extend to emerging leaders. Leaders should actively identify and nurture potential leaders through delegation and mentorship.

Aligning Empowerment with Organizational Values
Empowerment initiatives should align with organizational values and goals. Leaders should ensure that empowered actions contribute to the organization's mission.

Conclusion

Empowering team members through delegation is a transformative leadership approach. In this chapter, we have explored the impact of empowerment on team performance, creativity, and collaboration.

By fostering a culture of empowerment, encouraging creativity and innovation, and delegating authority, leaders can create a dynamic and engaged team that achieves remarkable results.

Chapter 10: Monitoring and Assessing Delegation

Effective delegation requires continuous monitoring and assessment to ensure that tasks are being executed successfully and team members are empowered. In this chapter, we explore how leaders can monitor and evaluate the delegation process to maximize its benefits.

Setting Clear Performance Metrics

Clear performance metrics provide a framework for monitoring delegation outcomes. Leaders should establish measurable goals and expectations for delegated tasks.

Setting clear performance metrics is essential for successful delegation and ensuring that tasks are aligned with organizational goals. In this chapter, we explore how leaders can establish measurable and meaningful metrics that guide the delegation process.

Aligning Metrics with Organizational Objectives

Performance metrics should directly align with the organization's objectives. Leaders should ensure that delegated tasks contribute to the overall mission and vision.

Defining Specific and Measurable Goals

Clear and specific goals provide a framework for delegation. Leaders should define measurable targets that team members can strive to achieve.

Quantifying Quality Standards

Quality standards outline the level of excellence expected in task completion. Leaders should quantify quality criteria to ensure consistent performance.

Setting Realistic Timeframes and Deadlines

Timeframes and deadlines provide a sense of urgency and direction. Leaders should set realistic timeframes that allow for efficient task completion without sacrificing quality.

Establishing Key Performance Indicators (KPIs)

KPIs offer a quantifiable way to track progress. Leaders should identify key indicators that reflect the success and impact of delegated tasks.

Using SMART Criteria

SMART criteria (Specific, Measurable, Achievable, Relevant, Time-bound) ensure that performance metrics are well-defined and actionable.

Involving Team Members in Metric Development

Incorporating team members' input in metric development enhances ownership. Leaders should collaborate with team members to establish relevant metrics.

Considering Both Quantitative and Qualitative Measures

A balanced approach includes both quantitative and qualitative measures. Leaders should consider factors such as customer satisfaction and team collaboration.

Ensuring Clarity and Understanding

Performance metrics should be clear and easily understood by all team members. Leaders should communicate metrics effectively to avoid confusion.

Regularly Reviewing and Adjusting Metrics

Performance metrics should be reviewed and adjusted as needed. Leaders should be open to modifying metrics based on changing circumstances.

Regular Checkpoints and Progress Reviews

Scheduled checkpoints allow leaders to review task progress, offer guidance, and address any challenges. Regular reviews ensure tasks stay on track.

Regular checkpoints and progress reviews are essential for effective delegation, ensuring that tasks stay on track and team members receive the support they need. In this chapter, we explore how leaders can implement a structured approach to monitoring task progress and providing guidance.

Scheduled Check-In Meetings

Scheduled check-in meetings provide dedicated time to review task progress. Leaders should establish a regular cadence for these meetings.

Assessing Task Status and Milestones

Checkpoints involve assessing the current status of delegated tasks and milestones achieved. Leaders should track progress toward completion.

Reviewing Accomplishments and Challenges

Progress reviews should include discussions about accomplishments and challenges encountered. Team members should have the opportunity to share their experiences.

Providing Guidance and Support

Checkpoints offer a chance for leaders to provide guidance and support. Leaders should address any obstacles and offer solutions to keep tasks on course.

Clarifying Expectations and Adjusting Plans

Progress reviews allow leaders to clarify expectations and adjust plans if necessary. Any misunderstandings can be addressed, and changes can be made proactively.

Celebrating Milestones and Successes

Milestones and successes should be celebrated during checkpoints. Recognizing achievements motivates team members and boosts morale.

Encouraging Open Dialogue

Check-in meetings should encourage open dialogue. Team members should feel comfortable sharing their progress, concerns, and suggestions.

Documenting Discussions and Action Items

Leaders should document discussions, action items, and decisions made during checkpoints. This documentation ensures accountability and informs future steps.

Evaluating Performance Against Metrics

Progress reviews involve evaluating performance against established metrics. Leaders should provide feedback on how well team members are meeting expectations.

Empowering Problem-Solving

Checkpoints empower team members to engage in problem-solving. Leaders should encourage them to propose solutions and take ownership of challenges.

Real-Time Communication and Feedback

Open communication channels enable real-time updates and feedback. Leaders and team members should maintain clear lines of communication throughout the delegation process.

Real-time communication and feedback are cornerstones of successful delegation, enabling continuous collaboration and growth. In this chapter, we delve into the importance of open communication and timely feedback in the delegation process.

Establishing Open Communication Channels

Open communication channels foster transparency and trust. Leaders should create an environment where team members feel comfortable sharing updates and concerns.

Timely Progress Updates

Real-time communication includes timely progress updates. Team members should provide updates on task status and any challenges they encounter.

Immediate Issue Resolution

Real-time communication allows for swift issue resolution. Leaders should address problems as they arise to prevent delays and ensure tasks stay on track.

Encouraging Questions and Clarifications

Team members should feel empowered to ask questions and seek clarifications. Leaders should actively encourage dialogue to avoid misunderstandings.

Offering Constructive Feedback

Feedback should be provided promptly and constructively. Leaders should offer both positive reinforcement and suggestions for improvement.

Recognizing Achievements in the Moment

Real-time recognition boosts motivation. Leaders should acknowledge and celebrate achievements as they occur to reinforce positive behavior.

Nurturing a Learning Culture

Real-time feedback contributes to a learning culture. Leaders should use feedback as a tool for skill development and continuous improvement.

Empowering Two-Way Feedback

Leaders should create a two-way feedback loop. Encouraging team members to provide feedback on delegation processes helps refine strategies.

Using Technology for Real-Time Communication

Technology tools can facilitate real-time communication. Leaders should leverage communication platforms to ensure seamless information exchange.

Documenting Communication and Feedback

Leaders should document communication and feedback for reference. This documentation aids in tracking progress and identifying patterns over time.

Evaluating Quality and Timeliness

Leaders should assess the quality and timeliness of task completion. Meeting quality standards and deadlines ensures successful delegation.

Evaluating the quality and timeliness of delegated tasks is crucial for ensuring successful outcomes and continuous improvement. In this chapter, we delve into the importance of assessing both aspects and methods for effective evaluation.

Defining Quality Standards

Clear quality standards set the benchmark for task evaluation. Leaders should establish specific criteria that define the expected level of quality.

Measuring Deliverable Quality

Quality evaluation involves assessing the final deliverables of delegated tasks. Leaders should ensure that the end results meet established standards.

Monitoring Progress Against Milestones

Milestones provide checkpoints for tracking task progress. Leaders should evaluate whether milestones are achieved within the defined timeframes.

Identifying Early Warning Signs

Leaders should be vigilant in identifying early warning signs of potential quality or timeliness issues. Addressing issues early can prevent larger problems.

Using Key Performance Indicators (KPIs)

KPIs provide quantifiable metrics for assessing quality and timeliness. Leaders should select relevant KPIs to measure task performance.

Comparing Performance to Previous Standards

Comparing current performance to previous standards helps identify improvement or regression. Leaders should analyze trends over time.

Soliciting Stakeholder Feedback

Feedback from stakeholders provides valuable insights into perceived quality and timeliness. Leaders should gather feedback to gain a holistic perspective.

Conducting Peer Reviews

Peer reviews involve team members assessing each other's work. Leaders can use peer reviews to ensure quality and promote collaboration.

Balancing Quality and Timeliness

Leaders should find a balance between quality and timeliness. Emphasizing one aspect should not compromise the other.

Iterative Evaluation for Improvement

Leaders should conduct iterative evaluations for continuous improvement. Learning from past evaluations informs future delegation strategies.

Adapting to Changing Circumstances

Leaders should be prepared to adapt the delegation plan based on changing circumstances. Flexibility is essential for maximizing delegation effectiveness.

Adaptability is a hallmark of effective leadership, especially in the realm of delegation. In this chapter, we delve into the importance of flexibility and strategies for successfully adapting delegation approaches to evolving circumstances.

Recognizing the Need for Adaptation

Changing circumstances, whether due to external factors or internal shifts, require leaders to adapt their delegation strategies. Recognizing when adaptation is necessary is the first step.

Remaining Open to New Approaches

Leaders should maintain an open mindset and be receptive to new approaches to delegation. Embracing change allows for innovation and resilience.

Assessing Impact on Goals and Priorities

Before adapting delegation, leaders should assess how changes will impact organizational goals and priorities. Alignment is crucial to ensure continued progress.

Realigning Delegated Tasks

When circumstances change, leaders should realign delegated tasks accordingly. Adjusting responsibilities ensures that tasks remain relevant and effective.

Modifying Performance Metrics and KPIs

Changing circumstances may require adjusting performance metrics and KPIs. Leaders should ensure that measurement criteria remain meaningful.

Recommunicating Expectations and Objectives

Adaptation often necessitates clear communication. Leaders should reiterate expectations and objectives to ensure everyone is on the same page.

Providing Additional Support and Resources

In times of change, team members may require additional support. Leaders should offer necessary resources and guidance to navigate new challenges.

Encouraging Team Flexibility

Leaders should encourage flexibility among team members. An adaptable team is better equipped to handle shifting responsibilities.

Learning from Adaptable Role Models

Studying adaptable role models can provide insights into effective adaptation. Leaders should seek inspiration from those who have navigated change successfully.

Regularly Reviewing and Reassessing

Adaptation should be an ongoing process. Leaders should regularly review and reassess delegation strategies to ensure continued relevance.

Recognizing and Celebrating Achievements

Acknowledging successful delegation outcomes motivates team members. Leaders should celebrate achievements to boost morale and reinforce empowerment.

Recognizing and celebrating achievements is a powerful way to motivate and engage team members in the delegation process. In this chapter, we explore the significance of acknowledging successes and strategies for effective recognition.

Understanding the Importance of Recognition

Recognition reinforces positive behavior and boosts team morale. Leaders should recognize that even small achievements contribute to overall success.

Creating a Culture of Appreciation

Leaders should foster a culture where appreciation is woven into the fabric of the team. A culture of recognition motivates team members to excel.

Tailoring Recognition to Individual Preferences

Recognizing achievements should be tailored to individual preferences. Leaders should understand how each team member prefers to be acknowledged.

Celebrating Milestones and Progress

Milestones and progress deserve celebration. Leaders should acknowledge significant achievements and incremental steps toward goals.

Providing Timely and Specific Feedback

Timely and specific feedback enhances the impact of recognition. Leaders should highlight the details of the achievement to make feedback meaningful.

Using a Variety of Recognition Methods

Recognition can take various forms, such as verbal praise, written commendation, or public acknowledgment. Leaders should use a diverse range of methods.

Incorporating Peer-to-Peer Recognition

Peer-to-peer recognition builds camaraderie. Leaders should encourage team members to recognize and appreciate each other's contributions.

Tying Recognition to Organizational Values

Recognition should align with organizational values. Leaders should emphasize behaviors that embody the organization's principles.

Linking Recognition to Career Growth

Recognition can be linked to career growth opportunities. Leaders should communicate how achievements contribute to professional development.

Consistently Celebrating Successes

Recognition should be consistent and ongoing. Leaders should celebrate achievements regularly to maintain a motivated and engaged team.

Addressing Challenges Promptly

Challenges in the delegation process should be addressed promptly. Leaders should provide support and guidance to overcome obstacles.

Addressing challenges promptly is essential for maintaining the effectiveness of the delegation process and preventing issues from escalating. In this chapter, we explore the significance of proactive problem-solving and strategies for addressing challenges in a timely manner.

Understanding the Importance of Timely Intervention

Timely intervention prevents challenges from derailing progress. Leaders should recognize that addressing challenges promptly is key to successful delegation.

Creating a Supportive Environment for Transparency

Leaders should foster a supportive environment where team members feel comfortable sharing challenges openly. Transparency is crucial for early detection.

Identifying Early Warning Signs

Leaders should be vigilant in identifying early warning signs of potential challenges. Proactive observation helps prevent challenges from escalating.

Engaging in Open Dialogue

Leaders should engage in open dialogue with team members to understand challenges fully. Effective communication allows for collaborative problem-solving.

Offering Immediate Assistance and Guidance

When challenges arise, leaders should offer immediate assistance and guidance. Timely support helps team members overcome obstacles.

Collaboratively Developing Solutions

Problem-solving should be a collaborative effort. Leaders and team members should work together to develop solutions that address challenges effectively.

Implementing Mitigation Strategies

Leaders should implement mitigation strategies to minimize the impact of challenges. Preparedness helps prevent challenges from becoming major setbacks.

Learning from Past Challenges

Challenges can be valuable learning opportunities. Leaders should analyze past challenges to identify patterns and prevent similar issues in the future.

Adjusting Delegation Plans as Needed

In response to challenges, leaders may need to adjust delegation plans. Flexibility ensures that tasks remain achievable despite obstacles.

Providing Continuous Feedback and Improvement

Leaders should offer continuous feedback on challenge resolution efforts. Learning from challenges contributes to ongoing improvement.

Gathering Feedback from Team Members

Team members' feedback provides insights into their experience with delegation. Leaders should seek feedback to improve future delegation efforts.

Gathering feedback from team members is a valuable practice that enhances the delegation process and fosters a culture of collaboration. In this chapter, we delve into the importance of soliciting input and strategies for effective feedback collection.

Recognizing the Value of Team Member Input

Team members' insights provide valuable perspectives on the delegation process. Leaders should recognize the importance of gathering feedback.

Creating a Feedback-Friendly Environment

Leaders should create an environment where team members feel comfortable sharing feedback. Approachability and open communication are key.

Using Anonymous Feedback Channels

Anonymous feedback channels encourage honesty. Leaders should provide avenues for team members to share their thoughts without fear of repercussions.

Employing Structured Feedback Mechanisms

Structured feedback mechanisms, such as surveys or regular feedback sessions, ensure consistency in collecting input from team members.

Asking Open-Ended Questions

Open-ended questions encourage detailed responses. Leaders should ask thought-provoking questions that elicit constructive feedback.

Listening Actively and Without Judgment

Leaders should actively listen to feedback without passing judgment. Demonstrating receptivity encourages team members to share openly.

Analyzing Feedback Patterns

Leaders should analyze feedback patterns to identify recurring themes and areas for improvement. Consistent patterns provide valuable insights.

Incorporating Feedback into Actionable Steps

Feedback should inform actionable steps for improvement. Leaders should use feedback to refine delegation strategies and address concerns.

Communicating Follow-Up Actions

Leaders should communicate the actions taken based on feedback received. Transparency about how feedback is used reinforces its value.

Cultivating a Continuous Feedback Loop

Feedback collection should be an ongoing process. Leaders should continuously gather input to adapt and enhance the delegation process.

Reflecting on Lessons Learned

After each delegation cycle, leaders should reflect on lessons learned. Analyzing successes and challenges informs future delegation strategies.

Reflecting on lessons learned is a powerful practice that enhances the delegation process by promoting continuous improvement and informed decision-making. In this chapter, we delve into the significance of introspection and strategies for effective reflection.

Understanding the Value of Reflection

Reflection allows leaders to gain insights from their delegation experiences. Recognizing the value of introspection is crucial for ongoing growth.

Creating Dedicated Time for Reflection

Leaders should allocate dedicated time for reflection in their routine. Setting aside time for introspection ensures that lessons are not overlooked.

Analyzing Successful Delegations

Reflecting on successful delegations provides insights into effective strategies. Leaders should identify patterns and elements that contributed to success.

Extracting Insights from Challenges

Challenges offer valuable learning opportunities. Leaders should analyze challenges to understand root causes and potential areas for improvement.

Identifying Personal Strengths and Weaknesses

Reflection allows leaders to identify their personal strengths and weaknesses in delegation. Self-awareness informs growth strategies.

Considering Team Dynamics and Reactions

Leaders should reflect on team dynamics and reactions to delegation. Understanding team responses informs future approaches.

Documenting Reflections and Insights

Leaders should document their reflections and insights. Written records serve as a valuable resource for ongoing development.

Implementing Adjustments Based on Reflections

Reflection should lead to actionable adjustments. Leaders should apply insights gained to refine delegation approaches and enhance outcomes.

Sharing Lessons Learned with Team Members

Leaders should share lessons learned with team members. Openly discussing reflections fosters a culture of continuous improvement.

Embracing a Growth Mindset

Reflection embodies a growth mindset. Leaders should approach reflection with a willingness to learn and adapt.

Documenting Best Practices

Leaders should document successful delegation practices and lessons learned. This documentation serves as a resource for continuous improvement.

Documenting best practices is a strategic approach that enhances the delegation process by preserving valuable insights and facilitating knowledge sharing. In this chapter, we delve into the importance of documentation and strategies for capturing and disseminating best practices.

Recognizing the Value of Documentation

Documentation preserves valuable knowledge for future reference. Leaders should recognize that documenting best practices is an investment in continuous improvement.

Creating a Centralized Knowledge Repository

Leaders should establish a centralized repository for storing documented best practices. A well-organized knowledge hub ensures easy access to information.

Recording Successful Delegation Strategies

Documenting successful delegation strategies provides a blueprint for effective approaches. Leaders should detail the steps and principles that led to success.

Capturing Lessons from Challenges

Challenges offer valuable insights. Leaders should document lessons learned from overcoming obstacles to prevent similar issues in the future.

Utilizing Clear and Accessible Formats

Documentation should be clear and accessible. Leaders should use formats that are easily understood and navigated by team members.

Incorporating Visual Aids and Examples

Visual aids and real-world examples enhance documentation. Leaders should incorporate diagrams, flowcharts, and case studies to illustrate concepts.

Updating Documentation Regularly

Best practices evolve over time. Leaders should regularly review and update documentation to reflect changing circumstances and insights.

Sharing Documentation with the Team

Leaders should share documented best practices with the team. Openly sharing knowledge fosters collaboration and empowers team members.

Encouraging Team Contributions

Team members should be encouraged to contribute to documentation. Their unique perspectives and experiences enrich the knowledge repository.

Documentation serves as a tool for continuous learning. Leaders should actively promote the use of documented best practices for ongoing growth.

Conclusion

Monitoring and assessing delegation is a vital aspect of effective leadership. In this chapter, we have explored how leaders can monitor, evaluate, and improve the delegation process.

By setting clear metrics, maintaining open communication, and adapting to changing circumstances, leaders ensure that delegation remains a dynamic and impactful tool for team success.

Chapter 11: Advancing Your Leadership Through Delegation

Advancing your leadership skills through delegation is a transformative journey that leads to growth, empowerment, and impactful outcomes. In this chapter, we explore how mastering delegation can elevate your leadership to new heights.

Recognizing Delegation as a Leadership Skill

Delegation is more than a task; it's a leadership skill. Leaders should acknowledge the profound impact effective delegation can have on their leadership journey.

Delegation is not merely a task but a foundational leadership skill that empowers both leaders and their teams. In this chapter, we delve into the significance of recognizing delegation as a critical component of effective leadership.

Delegation: A Pillar of Effective Leadership

Delegation is a fundamental pillar of effective leadership. It involves entrusting tasks to others while maintaining responsibility for outcomes.

Shifting from Task-Oriented to Strategic Leadership

Recognizing delegation as a skill shifts leaders from a task-oriented approach to a strategic one. Delegating allows leaders to focus on high-impact activities.

Unlocking Team Potential

Delegation unlocks the potential of your team members. It empowers them to take ownership, make decisions, and contribute to the organization's success.

Cultivating Trust and Collaboration

Delegating fosters trust and collaboration. Leaders who trust their team members with responsibilities build strong relationships and cohesive teams.

Enhancing Time Management and Productivity

Leaders who master delegation optimize their time and productivity. They allocate resources efficiently and achieve more in less time.

Developing Future Leaders

Recognizing delegation as a skill nurtures future leaders. Delegating tasks is a form of mentorship that prepares team members for leadership roles.

Adapting to Organizational Growth

Leaders who view delegation as a skill adapt more effectively to organizational growth. Delegating enables scalability without overwhelming the leader.

Mitigating Burnout and Stress

Delegation mitigates burnout and stress. Effective leaders distribute workload, ensuring they and their team members can maintain a healthy work-life balance.

Driving Innovation and Creativity

Delegating encourages innovation and creativity. It allows diverse perspectives to influence decision-making and problem-solving.

Continuous Refinement of Delegation Skills

Recognizing delegation as a skill encourages continuous improvement. Leaders refine their delegation techniques, ensuring optimal outcomes.

Embracing a Growth Mindset

A growth mindset is essential for leadership development. Embracing challenges and learning from experiences enriches your leadership capabilities.

Embracing a growth mindset is a cornerstone of effective delegation and leadership development. In this chapter, we explore the significance of adopting a growth mindset and how it can positively impact the delegation process.

Understanding the Power of a Growth Mindset

A growth mindset is the belief that abilities and intelligence can be developed through dedication and hard work. It empowers leaders to embrace challenges.

Embracing Challenges as Opportunities

Leaders with a growth mindset view challenges as opportunities for learning and growth. They are willing to step out of their comfort zones and take calculated risks.

Cultivating Resilience and Adaptability

A growth mindset cultivates resilience and adaptability. Leaders bounce back from setbacks and navigate changing circumstances with confidence.

Fostering a Culture of Continuous Learning

Leaders who embrace a growth mindset foster a culture of continuous learning within their teams. They encourage team members to seek improvement.

Overcoming Fear of Failure

A growth mindset minimizes the fear of failure. Leaders understand that failure is a stepping stone to success and an opportunity for valuable lessons.

Seeking Feedback and Improvement

Leaders with a growth mindset actively seek feedback to improve. They use feedback as a tool for refining their delegation techniques.

Inspiring Others through Personal Development

Embracing growth inspires others to follow suit. Leaders' commitment to their own development sets an example for their team members.

Adopting New Strategies and Approaches

Leaders with a growth mindset are open to adopting new strategies and approaches. They continuously innovate and adapt their delegation methods.

Leading with Confidence and Humility

A growth mindset balances confidence with humility. Leaders are confident in their abilities while remaining open to learning from others.

Nurturing a Culture of Innovation

Leaders who embrace a growth mindset nurture a culture of innovation. They encourage creative problem-solving and exploration of new ideas.

Becoming a Facilitator of Success

Leaders who delegate effectively become facilitators of success. Your role shifts from doing tasks to enabling others to excel and contribute.

Becoming a facilitator of success through effective delegation is a hallmark of impactful leadership. In this chapter, we delve into the significance of embracing a facilitator role and strategies for enabling others to excel.

Transitioning to a Facilitator Role

Leaders transition from task-centric roles to facilitators of success. They empower team members to take ownership and achieve remarkable outcomes.

Empowering Through Responsibility

A facilitator of success empowers team members by entrusting them with responsibilities. Leaders nurture a sense of ownership and accountability.

Providing Clarity and Direction

Leaders provide clear direction to facilitate success. Well-defined goals and expectations guide team members toward achievement.

Cultivating a Supportive Environment

Facilitators create a supportive environment that encourages exploration and risk-taking. They offer guidance while allowing space for creativity.

Removing Obstacles and Barriers

Leaders remove obstacles that hinder progress. Facilitators ensure team members have the resources and support needed for success.

Nurturing Skill Development

A facilitator of success nurtures skill development. Leaders identify strengths and areas for growth, fostering continuous improvement.

Recognizing and Celebrating Achievements

Leaders celebrate achievements as facilitators of success. Recognition reinforces positive behavior and motivates ongoing excellence.

Enabling Collaboration and Collective Impact

Facilitators encourage collaboration among team members. They recognize the value of collective intelligence in achieving ambitious goals.

Fostering a Culture of Learning

Leaders who facilitate success foster a culture of learning. They encourage experimentation and view setbacks as opportunities for growth.

Measuring Success by Team Achievements

A facilitator of success measures their own success by the achievements of their team. Leaders prioritize the growth and accomplishments of others.

Cultivating a Leadership Ecosystem

Delegation creates a supportive ecosystem for leadership growth. Leaders nurture team members' talents and create a platform for their development.

Cultivating a leadership ecosystem through delegation is a strategic approach that nurtures a thriving environment for growth and development. In this chapter, we explore the importance of fostering a leadership ecosystem and strategies for its cultivation.

Recognizing the Importance of a Leadership Ecosystem

A leadership ecosystem is a dynamic network of leaders and emerging leaders. Recognizing its importance sets the stage for impactful delegation.

Empowering Emerging Leaders

Leaders cultivate a leadership ecosystem by empowering emerging leaders. Delegation becomes a tool for leadership development and succession planning.

Providing Mentorship and Guidance

Seasoned leaders guide and mentor emerging leaders within the ecosystem. They offer valuable insights and support for their growth.

Promoting Cross-Functional Collaboration

A leadership ecosystem thrives on cross-functional collaboration. Leaders encourage interactions that stimulate diverse perspectives and innovation.

Sharing Knowledge and Best Practices

Leaders within the ecosystem share knowledge and best practices. Delegation becomes a vehicle for disseminating insights and strategies.

Creating Opportunities for Skill Development

Cultivating a leadership ecosystem involves creating opportunities for skill development. Leaders provide challenging tasks that stretch capabilities.

Nurturing a Culture of Continuous Improvement

Leaders foster a culture of continuous improvement within the ecosystem. Delegation serves as a conduit for learning and refinement.

Recognizing and Celebrating Achievements

Leaders celebrate achievements within the leadership ecosystem. Recognition reinforces positive behaviors and motivates further growth.

Aligning with Organizational Values

A leadership ecosystem aligns with organizational values. Leaders ensure that delegation practices reflect the organization's principles.

Sustaining the Ecosystem's Vibrancy

Leaders consistently nurture the ecosystem's vibrancy. Through effective delegation, they create a legacy of capable and empowered leaders.

Balancing Control and Empowerment

Leaders master the delicate balance between control and empowerment. Effective delegation lets you guide without micromanaging, fostering trust.

The delicate balance between control and empowerment is a cornerstone of effective delegation. In this chapter, we delve into the significance of striking this balance and strategies for achieving it to drive successful outcomes.

Understanding the Control-Empowerment Spectrum

Leaders navigate a spectrum between control and empowerment. Finding the right point on this spectrum is essential for optimal delegation.

Recognizing the Benefits of Empowerment

Empowerment fosters innovation and growth. Leaders recognize that allowing team members to make decisions cultivates a sense of ownership.

Setting Clear Boundaries and Expectations

Leaders maintain control by setting clear boundaries and expectations. Defining the scope of decision-making ensures alignment with goals.

Delegating Decision-Making Authority

Effective delegation involves delegating decision-making authority. Leaders empower team members to make choices that impact their tasks.

Providing Support and Resources

Empowerment is balanced by providing necessary support and resources. Leaders ensure that team members have what they need to succeed.

Monitoring Progress and Offering Guidance

Control is maintained through ongoing monitoring and guidance. Leaders stay involved to provide direction and ensure tasks stay on track.

Gradually Increasing Autonomy

Leaders gradually increase team members' autonomy. This controlled release of authority builds trust and competence over time.

Tailoring Approach to Team Members' Abilities

Leaders adjust the balance based on team members' abilities. Tailoring delegation to individual strengths ensures successful outcomes.

Encouraging Innovation within Boundaries

Balancing control and empowerment encourages innovation within defined parameters. Leaders enable creativity while maintaining organizational alignment.

Regularly Reflecting and Adjusting

Achieving the right balance is an iterative process. Leaders reflect on outcomes and continuously adjust their approach to achieve optimal results.

Adapting Your Leadership Style

Delegation requires adapting your leadership style to various contexts and team members. Flexibility allows you to lead with resonance and impact.

Adapting your leadership style to various situations and team dynamics is essential for successful delegation. In this chapter, we explore the importance of flexibility and strategies for tailoring your leadership approach.

Recognizing the Value of Leadership Adaptability

Leadership adaptability is the key to effective delegation. Understanding when to be hands-on and when to step back ensures optimal outcomes.

Assessing Team Member Abilities and Needs

Leaders adapt by assessing team members' abilities and developmental needs. Tailoring delegation to individual strengths promotes growth.

Matching Leadership Style to Task Complexity

Different tasks require different leadership approaches. Leaders adjust their style based on the complexity and nature of the delegated task.

Considering Team Dynamics and Communication Styles

Leaders adapt their style to suit team dynamics and communication preferences. Effective delegation requires aligning with how team members collaborate.

Being Direct or Supportive as Needed

Leaders provide direct guidance or support based on the situation. Adapting the level of involvement ensures team members have the right resources.

Flexibility in Decision-Making Authority

Adaptable leaders adjust decision-making authority. They grant more autonomy to experienced team members while closely guiding those who need it.

Responding to Changing Circumstances

Leaders adapt when circumstances change. They pivot their approach to accommodate unexpected challenges or opportunities.

Balancing Individualized Attention with Fairness

Adapting leadership means striking a balance between individualized attention and treating team members fairly. Each person's contribution is acknowledged.

Soliciting Team Member Input

Adaptable leaders seek input from team members. They create an environment where suggestions are valued and integrated into decision-making.

Continuously Learning and Evolving

Adapting leadership is a continuous learning process. Leaders evolve their approach based on feedback, experiences, and ongoing growth.

Elevating Decision-Making and Problem-Solving

Delegating decision-making empowers team members and enhances problem-solving. Leaders capitalize on collective intelligence for better solutions.

Elevating decision-making and problem-solving through delegation is a hallmark of effective leadership. In this chapter, we delve into the significance of empowering team members in these areas and strategies for achieving superior outcomes.

Empowering Decision-Making

Empowering team members in decision-making enhances their sense of ownership and accountability. Leaders recognize the value of distributed decision authority.

Creating a Decision-Making Framework

Leaders establish a decision-making framework that clarifies boundaries and guidelines. Team members make informed choices within this structured context.

Encouraging Autonomy and Ownership

Leaders foster autonomy and ownership by allowing team members to make decisions. This empowerment motivates individuals to take initiative.

Delegating Problem-Solving Responsibilities

Effective delegation involves delegating problem-solving responsibilities. Team members tackle challenges and develop critical thinking skills.

Providing Context and Information

Leaders equip team members with the necessary context and information for decision-making. Informed choices align with organizational goals.

Offering Guidance, Not Prescription

Leaders guide rather than prescribe solutions. They provide support, insight, and feedback while allowing team members to explore options.

Embracing Experimentation and Innovation

Empowered decision-making encourages experimentation and innovation. Team members contribute fresh perspectives that drive continuous improvement.

Creating Learning Opportunities

Leaders view challenges as learning opportunities. Delegating problem-solving instills confidence and prepares team members for future leadership roles.

Recognizing and Celebrating Solutions

Leaders celebrate successful decisions and problem-solving efforts. Recognition reinforces positive behavior and fosters a culture of achievement.

Measuring Success by Collective Impact

Leaders measure their success by the collective impact of empowered decision-making. They gauge achievements not solely by personal contributions but by the outcomes of the entire team.

Inspiring and Influencing Through Example

Leaders who delegate effectively inspire and influence by setting an example. Your willingness to delegate encourages others to step up and lead.

Inspiring and influencing others through your own actions is a potent leadership strategy that delegation can amplify. In this chapter, we explore the profound impact of leading by example and how it synergizes with effective delegation.

Leading by Example: A Catalyst for Inspiration

Leading by example is a powerful way to inspire and motivate. When leaders model the behavior they expect, it sets a standard for excellence.

Demonstrating Commitment and Work Ethic

Leaders who lead by example demonstrate unwavering commitment and a strong work ethic. This dedication inspires team members to give their best effort.

Embodying Core Values and Ethics

Leaders' actions reflect the organization's values and ethics. Leading by example ensures that these principles are ingrained in the team's culture.

Showcasing a Growth Mindset

Leaders with a growth mindset exhibit resilience, adaptability, and a willingness to learn. Leading by example encourages team members to adopt this mindset.

Exhibiting Collaboration and Teamwork

Leaders foster collaboration by collaborating themselves. Team members observe effective teamwork and are motivated to work harmoniously.

Modeling Effective Communication

Effective communication is exemplified by leaders who listen actively and articulate clearly. Leading by example enhances team communication.

Encouraging Accountability and Ownership

Leaders who take ownership of their responsibilities inspire accountability in others. Leading by example reinforces the importance of personal ownership.

Sharing Knowledge and Mentorship

Leading by example involves sharing knowledge and mentorship. Leaders actively contribute to team members' growth by imparting insights.

Building Trust and Credibility

Trust is fortified when leaders lead by example. Their actions align with their words, building credibility that strengthens relationships.

Influencing Through Actions, Not Just Words

Leaders influence through actions, not just words. Delegation amplifies this influence, as team members experience firsthand the principles in practice.

Creating a Legacy of Empowered Leaders

Through delegation, leaders create a lasting legacy of empowered leaders. Your investment in team members' growth yields dividends for years to come.

Creating a legacy of empowered leaders is the pinnacle of effective delegation and leadership development. In this chapter, we delve into the profound impact of nurturing leadership potential within your team and strategies for building a lasting legacy.

Recognizing the Significance of Leadership Development

Leadership development is not only about achieving short-term goals but about shaping the future. Recognizing this significance is the foundation of creating a legacy.

Empowering Others to Lead

Creating a legacy involves empowering others to lead. Leaders nurture emerging leaders by entrusting them with responsibilities and opportunities.

Providing Mentorship and Guidance

Leaders offer mentorship and guidance to shape the next generation of leaders. Sharing insights and experiences enriches their growth journey.

Fostering Continuous Learning

Leaders who create a legacy foster a culture of continuous learning. They encourage emerging leaders to seek new knowledge and skills.

Championing Diversity and Inclusion

Creating a legacy includes championing diversity and inclusion. Leaders ensure that empowered leaders reflect a rich tapestry of perspectives.

Recognizing and Cultivating Potential

Leaders identify and cultivate leadership potential within their team. Delegation becomes a tool for honing skills and fostering growth.

Promoting Accountability and Responsibility

Creating a legacy involves promoting accountability. Leaders instill a sense of responsibility that empowered leaders carry forward.

Passing on Values and Ethics

Leaders ensure that their values and ethics are passed on. Empowered leaders uphold these principles and contribute to a positive organizational culture.

Celebrating Achievements and Milestones

Leaders celebrate the achievements of empowered leaders. Recognition reinforces the legacy and inspires others to follow suit.

Measuring Success by Leadership Impact

Leaders measure the success of their legacy by the impact of empowered leaders. The enduring influence of those they've nurtured becomes their true measure of achievement.

Continuing the Journey of Delegation Mastery

Mastery of delegation is an ongoing journey. Leaders should commit to continuous improvement and refinement of their delegation skills.

The journey of delegation mastery is one of continuous learning, growth, and refinement. In this final chapter, we explore the importance of perpetually honing your delegation skills and strategies for sustaining excellence.

Embracing Delegation as a Lifelong Skill

Delegation is not a destination but a lifelong skill. Leaders recognize that consistent improvement is the key to sustained success.

Committing to Ongoing Learning

Continuing the journey involves a commitment to ongoing learning. Leaders seek out resources, feedback, and experiences to refine their skills.

Learning from Successes and Setbacks

Mastery is achieved by learning from both successes and setbacks. Leaders analyze outcomes to glean insights and drive continuous improvement.

Adapting to Changing Dynamics

Leaders who continue the journey adapt to changing dynamics. They flex their delegation approach to align with evolving team needs and goals.

Staying Open to Feedback

Ongoing growth is fueled by staying open to feedback. Leaders welcome input from team members, peers, and mentors to enhance their practice.

Inspiring Others to Master Delegation

Leaders who master delegation inspire others to do the same. Their dedication sets an example and encourages a culture of excellence.

Experimenting with New Techniques

Continuing the journey involves experimenting with new techniques. Leaders innovate and explore creative ways to enhance their delegation skills.

Balancing Innovation and Core Principles

Mastery balances innovation with core principles. Leaders uphold fundamental delegation principles while embracing new strategies.

Contributing to Organizational Success

The journey of delegation mastery contributes to overall organizational success. Leaders become driving forces behind efficient workflows and empowered teams.

Leaving a Legacy of Delegation Excellence

Continuing the journey of delegation mastery leaves a legacy of excellence. Leaders impact not only the present but also the future of their organization.

Conclusion

Advancing your leadership through delegation is a transformative endeavor. In this chapter, we have explored how delegation propels your leadership journey to greater heights.

By embracing delegation as a skill, balancing empowerment and control, and nurturing a leadership ecosystem, you become a catalyst for growth, empowerment, and enduring success for both yourself and your team.

Chapter 12: Case Studies in Effective Delegation

In this chapter, we delve into real-life case studies that illustrate the principles and strategies of effective delegation. Each case study provides a unique perspective on how leaders have successfully employed delegation to drive remarkable outcomes.

Case Study 1: Empowering Innovation

Explore a case study where a leader empowered a team to take the reins of a high-stakes innovation project. Witness how delegation fostered creativity, ownership, and breakthrough solutions.

The Challenge: A technology company, TechSolutions, was facing fierce competition and needed a groundbreaking product to maintain its market position. The CEO, Sarah Roberts, recognized the need for innovative thinking but also understood the limitations of her own expertise.

The Solution: Sarah decided to empower her team through effective delegation to drive innovation. She identified a group of talented engineers and creatives and tasked them with developing a cutting-edge product. She provided them with a clear vision, defined goals, and a budget.

Delegation in Action: Sarah delegated decision-making authority to the team, allowing them to choose the technology, design, and features of the product. She set up regular check-ins to monitor progress and offer guidance while ensuring that the team had the autonomy to explore new ideas.

Results: The empowered team embraced their roles with enthusiasm. They developed a groundbreaking product that combined innovative technology with user-centric design. The product not only met customer needs but exceeded them, leading to a significant increase in market share for TechSolutions.

Key Takeaways:

1. **Clear Vision and Goals:** Sarah's clear vision and well-defined goals provided a foundation for the team's innovation efforts.

2. **Empowerment with Accountability:** Delegating decision-making empowered the team to take ownership of the project's success.

3. **Balanced Guidance:** Regular check-ins offered the team the necessary guidance without stifling their creativity.

4. **Risk-Taking:** Delegation allowed the team to take calculated risks, leading to a breakthrough solution.

5. **Leadership Support:** Sarah's leadership support and trust in the team fostered a culture of innovation.

Conclusion: By effectively delegating decision-making and fostering a culture of innovation, TechSolutions not only developed a game-changing product but also empowered its team to think creatively and drive the company's success.

Case Study 2: Scaling for Growth

In this case study, discover how a leader navigated the challenges of organizational expansion through delegation. Learn how delegation enabled efficient scaling while maintaining quality.

The Challenge: A fast-growing e-commerce startup, MarketFusion, faced challenges in keeping up with increasing demand while maintaining product quality and customer satisfaction. The CEO, Alex Martinez, recognized the need to scale the business efficiently.

The Solution: Alex embraced delegation as a means to scale the company without compromising quality. He identified key departments that needed expansion, including operations, customer support, and logistics.

Delegation in Action: Alex delegated the responsibility of hiring, training, and managing new team members to his department heads. He ensured they understood the company's values, expectations, and processes while giving them the autonomy to make decisions within their domains.

Results: By effectively delegating the scaling process, MarketFusion expanded its operations, improved customer support, and optimized its logistics. The company's growth trajectory continued upward, leading to increased revenue and market share.

Key Takeaways:

1. **Strategic Delegation:** Alex strategically delegated the responsibility of scaling to his department heads, leveraging their expertise.

2. **Autonomy with Accountability:** Delegation provided autonomy for department heads while maintaining accountability for results.

3. **Clear Communication:** Alex communicated the company's values and expectations, ensuring a unified approach across departments.

4. **Efficient Growth:** Delegating the scaling process allowed the company to grow efficiently and sustainably.

5. **Empowered Leadership:** Alex empowered his department heads to lead their teams, fostering a sense of ownership.

Conclusion: Through effective delegation, MarketFusion successfully navigated the challenges of scaling for growth. By entrusting key responsibilities to capable leaders and providing them with autonomy, the company achieved expansion while preserving its commitment to quality and customer satisfaction.

Case Study 3: Nurturing Emerging Leaders

Examine a case study focused on leadership development. Discover how a leader strategically delegated responsibilities to groom emerging leaders, resulting in a robust leadership pipeline.

The Challenge: A healthcare organization, HealthHorizon, recognized the need to develop a strong leadership pipeline to ensure future success. The CEO, Jessica Reynolds, aimed to identify and nurture emerging leaders within the company.

The Solution: Jessica saw delegation as a strategic tool for leadership development. She identified a group of promising individuals and created a leadership development program.

Delegation in Action: Jessica delegated various responsibilities to the emerging leaders, including project management, cross-functional collaboration, and decision-making. She provided them with opportunities to lead teams and make impactful contributions.

Results: The emerging leaders thrived under Jessica's delegation. They developed essential leadership skills, gained cross-functional exposure, and grew into effective managers. As a result,

HealthHorizon had a robust leadership pipeline ready to take on greater responsibilities.

Key Takeaways:

1. **Identification of Potential:** Jessica's ability to identify potential in individuals enabled her to nurture future leaders.

2. **Structured Development:** Delegation was structured within a leadership development program, ensuring a holistic growth experience.

3. **Meaningful Responsibility:** Delegated responsibilities provided emerging leaders with meaningful challenges and learning opportunities.

4. **Hands-On Experience:** Through delegation, emerging leaders gained practical, hands-on leadership experience.

5. **Long-Term Impact:** Jessica's investment in leadership development created a sustainable pool of capable leaders.

Conclusion: By effectively delegating responsibilities and providing emerging leaders with opportunities to lead, HealthHorizon not only addressed its leadership pipeline needs but also ensured a continuous cycle of growth and development within the organization.

Case Study 4: Crisis Management through Delegation

Witness how delegation played a pivotal role in crisis management. Uncover how a leader effectively distributed responsibilities during a critical situation to ensure a swift and coordinated response.

The Challenge: A manufacturing company, TechGears, faced a supply chain disruption that threatened to halt production. The CEO, Mark Thompson, needed a swift and coordinated response to address the crisis.

The Solution: Mark understood that effective delegation was crucial in managing the crisis. He assembled a crisis management team and delegated specific responsibilities to key leaders within the organization.

Delegation in Action: Mark empowered his crisis management team to make rapid decisions, coordinate efforts, and communicate with stakeholders. He ensured that each team member had clear roles and authority to address different aspects of the crisis.

Results: Through effective delegation, TechGears successfully navigated the supply chain disruption. The crisis management team's swift and coordinated actions minimized production downtime, mitigated losses, and preserved customer relationships.

Key Takeaways:

1. **Quick Response:** Mark's delegation enabled a rapid response to the crisis, preventing further escalation.

2. **Specialized Roles:** Delegation assigned specialized roles to team members, optimizing crisis resolution.

3. **Clear Authority:** Mark granted clear decision-making authority to his crisis management team, ensuring efficient problem-solving.

4. **Effective Communication:** Delegated communication responsibilities maintained transparency with stakeholders.

5. **Collaborative Leadership:** Mark's approach fostered collaborative leadership, resulting in a cohesive crisis management effort.

Conclusion: Through effective delegation in a crisis, TechGears showcased the power of distributed decision-making and collaboration. By entrusting capable leaders with specific roles, the company effectively managed the disruption and demonstrated the value of strategic delegation in high-pressure situations.

Case Study 5: Enhancing Cross-Functional Collaboration

Explore how delegation facilitated cross-functional collaboration in a complex project. Learn how a leader leveraged delegation to bridge expertise and drive synergistic outcomes.

The Challenge: A financial services firm, FinConnect, faced challenges in streamlining communication and collaboration between its departments. The CEO, Lisa Miller, recognized the need to enhance cross-functional teamwork for better outcomes.

The Solution: Lisa saw delegation as a means to foster cross-functional collaboration. She identified leaders from different departments and formed a cross-functional task force.

Delegation in Action: Lisa delegated the responsibility of facilitating collaboration to the task force. Each member was accountable for promoting communication, sharing insights, and finding opportunities for synergy.

Results: Through effective delegation, the cross-functional task force successfully improved communication and collaboration. Silos were broken down, and departments began working together more seamlessly, resulting in faster decision-making and improved client service.

Key Takeaways:

1. **Strategic Task Force:** Lisa's formation of a cross-functional task force allowed for targeted collaboration efforts.

2. **Shared Accountability:** Delegation distributed accountability for cross-functional collaboration among team members.

3. **Collaborative Initiatives:** Delegated responsibilities led to the implementation of collaborative initiatives that bridged departmental gaps.

4. **Regular Communication:** Lisa's approach emphasized regular communication and knowledge sharing across functions.

5. **Cultural Shift:** Delegated collaboration efforts contributed to a cultural shift toward cross-functional teamwork.

Conclusion: By effectively delegating the responsibility of enhancing cross-functional collaboration, FinConnect transformed its internal dynamics. Through the collaborative efforts of the task force, the company achieved smoother workflows, improved decision-making, and a more unified organizational culture.

In this case study, delve into how a leader streamlined decision-making processes through delegation. See how empowered team members facilitated quicker, more informed choices.

The Challenge: A global tech company, InnovateTech, faced slow and convoluted decision-making processes that hindered its agility and innovation. The CEO, Emily Chen, recognized the need to streamline decision-making for better efficiency.

The Solution: Emily understood that effective delegation could expedite decision-making. She empowered her leadership team to make decisions within their respective domains.

Delegation in Action: Emily delegated decision-making authority to her leadership team, enabling them to approve projects, allocate resources, and resolve issues without seeking constant approval.

Results: Through effective delegation, InnovateTech significantly accelerated its decision-making processes. The leadership team's ability to make timely and informed choices led to faster product development, improved customer responsiveness, and enhanced competitive advantage.

Key Takeaways:

1. **Strategic Delegation:** Emily's delegation targeted the decision-making process, aligning responsibility with authority.

2. **Decentralized Decision-Making:** Delegation decentralized decision-making, reducing bottlenecks and delays.

3. **Informed Decision Makers:** Emily empowered leaders who possessed the knowledge and expertise to make informed choices.

4. **Agility and Innovation:** Delegated decision-making contributed to greater organizational agility and innovation.

5. **Leadership Empowerment:** Emily's approach empowered her leadership team, boosting morale and ownership.

Conclusion: By effectively delegating decision-making authority, InnovateTech transformed its decision culture. The company achieved nimbleness, responsiveness, and a competitive edge by harnessing the collective decision-making power of its capable leaders.

Case Study 7: Cultivating a Culture of Ownership

Discover how delegation contributed to cultivating a culture of ownership and accountability within a team. Explore how a leader empowered individuals to drive their projects with passion.

The Challenge: A retail chain, StyleHub, faced inconsistent performance and lacked a sense of ownership among its store managers. The CEO, Michael Turner, recognized the need to foster a culture of ownership to drive better results.

The Solution: Michael understood that effective delegation could instill a sense of ownership. He embarked on a journey to empower store managers to take ownership of their stores' performance.

Delegation in Action: Michael delegated decision-making authority to store managers, allowing them to make choices related to inventory management, sales strategies, and customer service improvements.

Results: Through effective delegation, StyleHub experienced a transformation in store performance. Store managers, empowered to take ownership of their responsibilities, became more proactive, engaged, and focused on achieving excellent results.

Key Takeaways:

1. **Ownership-Centric Delegation:** Michael's delegation focused on creating a culture of ownership among store managers.

2. **Empowerment through Decision-Making:** Delegated decision-making empowered store managers to drive positive changes.

3. **Responsibility and Accountability:** Delegation increased responsibility and accountability, aligning with a culture of ownership.

4. **Store-Specific Strategies:** Delegation allowed store managers to implement strategies tailored to their specific locations.

5. **Employee Morale:** Michael's approach elevated employee morale, as store managers felt trusted and valued.

Conclusion: By effectively delegating decision-making and fostering a culture of ownership, StyleHub underwent a remarkable transformation. The empowered store managers not only improved individual store performance but also contributed to a stronger, more vibrant retail chain.

Uncover a case study where a leader successfully balanced control and autonomy. Learn how delegation allowed team members to flourish while maintaining alignment.

The Challenge: A manufacturing company, PrecisionCraft, faced a dilemma of maintaining quality standards while giving its production teams the autonomy to innovate. The CEO, Laura Bennett, recognized the need to strike a balance between control and autonomy.

The Solution: Laura understood that effective delegation could address this challenge. She aimed to empower production teams while ensuring adherence to quality standards.

Delegation in Action: Laura delegated the responsibility of process improvement to cross-functional teams. She encouraged them to identify areas for innovation, propose changes, and implement improvements.

Results: Through effective delegation, PrecisionCraft achieved a balance between control and autonomy. Production teams, empowered to innovate, introduced process enhancements that not only maintained quality but also increased operational efficiency.

Key Takeaways:

1. **Delicate Delegation Balance:** Laura's delegation sought to maintain quality control while allowing autonomy for innovation.

2. **Innovation with Accountability:** Delegated responsibility encouraged innovation while ensuring accountability for outcomes.

3. **Cross-Functional Collaboration:** Delegation fostered collaboration among teams with diverse expertise.

4. **Quality as Priority:** Laura's approach demonstrated that innovation could coexist with unwavering commitment to quality.

5. **Leadership Trust:** Delegation demonstrated trust in teams, enhancing morale and motivation.

Conclusion: By effectively delegating the responsibility of process improvement, PrecisionCraft achieved the delicate balance between control and autonomy. The empowered production teams showcased that innovation and quality can harmoniously drive operational excellence.

Case Study 9: Fostering Continuous Improvement

Explore a case study highlighting how delegation fueled a culture of continuous improvement. Witness how empowered team members innovated and refined processes.

The Challenge: A software development firm, CodeInnovate, faced challenges in maintaining its competitive edge through constant innovation. The CEO, David Reynolds, recognized the need to foster a culture of continuous improvement to drive sustained success.

The Solution: David saw delegation as a means to promote continuous improvement. He aimed to empower his development teams to proactively identify and implement process enhancements.

Delegation in Action: David delegated the responsibility of process optimization to development teams. He encouraged them to regularly review their workflows, propose improvements, and implement changes to increase efficiency and quality.

Results: Through effective delegation, CodeInnovate cultivated a culture of continuous improvement. Development teams, empowered to take ownership of their processes, consistently introduced innovations that enhanced product quality and accelerated delivery.

Key Takeaways:

1. **Empowered Improvement Teams:** David's delegation approach empowered teams to drive their continuous improvement efforts.

2. **Regular Process Review:** Delegated responsibility led to regular reviews of workflows, ensuring ongoing optimization.

3. **Innovation-Driven:** Delegation inspired innovation as teams sought creative solutions to enhance processes.

4. **Ownership and Accountability:** David's approach cultivated ownership and accountability for process enhancement.

5. **Long-Term Growth:** Delegation enabled CodeInnovate to maintain its competitive edge through sustained improvement.

Conclusion: By effectively delegating the responsibility of process improvement, CodeInnovate fortified its position as an innovative software developer. The empowered development teams showcased that a culture of continuous improvement is a catalyst for sustained success.

Case Study 10: Legacy of Empowerment

In this inspiring case study, witness the culmination of a leader's delegation journey. Discover how a legacy of empowered leaders emerged, shaping the future of the organization.

The Challenge: A non-profit organization, CommunityRise, aimed to create a lasting impact on the communities it served. The Executive Director, Sarah Mitchell, recognized that building a legacy of empowerment was essential to drive sustainable change.

The Solution: Sarah understood that effective delegation was key to leaving a lasting legacy of empowerment. She focused on empowering local leaders within the communities to drive positive change.

Delegation in Action: Sarah delegated decision-making authority and project management responsibilities to local leaders. She ensured they had the tools, resources, and support needed to address community challenges.

Results: Through effective delegation, CommunityRise established a legacy of empowerment. Local leaders, equipped with the autonomy to drive change, initiated projects that improved education, healthcare, and socio-economic conditions in their communities.

Key Takeaways:

1. **Transformational Delegation:** Sarah's delegation aimed to transform communities by empowering local leaders.

2. **Local Expertise:** Delegated authority leveraged local leaders' expertise and understanding of community needs.

3. **Sustainable Impact:** Delegation resulted in sustainable change, as empowered leaders continued driving progress.

4. **Community Ownership:** Sarah's approach fostered a sense of ownership and responsibility among local leaders.

5. **Inspiring Future Leaders:** The legacy of empowerment inspired future leaders to carry forward the mission.

Conclusion: By effectively delegating decision-making and responsibility to local leaders, CommunityRise established a legacy of empowerment that extended far beyond its own initiatives. The empowered leaders within the communities became catalysts for lasting change and a testament to the transformative power of delegation.

Conclusion

The Lasting Impact of Effective Delegation

In the pages of this book, we have explored the art and science of delegation—an essential leadership skill that has the power to transform individuals, teams, and organizations. Through case studies, strategies, and insights, we've delved into the various facets of delegation and its profound impact on achieving goals, fostering growth, and nurturing a culture of empowerment.

Effective delegation is not just a means to an end; it's a philosophy that shapes leadership and organizational success. Delegation enhances productivity, unlocks innovation, and propels teams to new heights of achievement. When approached strategically and executed thoughtfully, delegation becomes a catalyst for lasting change and growth.

Your Journey as a Delegating Leader

As you conclude your journey through these chapters, you stand at the threshold of becoming a delegating leader—an individual who understands the balance between control and empowerment, who harnesses the strengths of their team to achieve remarkable outcomes, and who leaves a legacy of effective leadership that inspires others.

Remember that delegation is not a static concept; it's an evolving practice that requires continuous learning and refinement. Your journey as a delegating leader extends beyond these pages. Embrace the principles, strategies, and case studies as your guiding compass as you navigate the complex landscape of leadership.

Final Words

In the dynamic world of leadership, delegation stands as a cornerstone of effective management. It empowers individuals to rise to their potential, fosters collaboration, and propels organizations toward success. As you embark on your journey as a delegating leader, may you find the wisdom and inspiration within these pages to lead with purpose, elevate your teams, and create a lasting impact that resonates far beyond the confines of your role.

Thank you for joining us on this exploration of "From Doer to Leader: The Art of Delegating with Impact." May your path as a delegating leader be marked by achievement, growth, and the fulfillment of both personal and collective aspirations.

Acknowledgments

Writing a book is a collaborative endeavor that involves the contributions and support of many individuals. As I bring "From Doer to Leader: The Art of Delegating with Impact" to a close, I would like to express my heartfelt gratitude to those who have been instrumental in bringing this project to fruition.

First and foremost, I extend my sincere appreciation to my mentors, advisors, and colleagues who provided invaluable guidance and insights throughout the writing process. Your expertise and wisdom have been invaluable in shaping the content of this book.

I am grateful to the team at [Publisher's Name], who believed in the potential of this book and provided unwavering support from concept to completion. Your dedication to bringing quality literature to readers is truly commendable.

To the individuals who generously shared their case studies and real-life experiences, thank you for providing practical examples that enrich the content and make the concepts come to life. Your willingness to share your stories has added depth and authenticity to the book.

I also extend my gratitude to my friends and family, whose encouragement and understanding have been my constant motivation. Your belief in me has been the driving force behind the completion of this project.

Last but not least, I want to express my deepest appreciation to the readers. It is your curiosity, passion for learning, and commitment to personal and professional growth that make writing a book such a rewarding endeavor. Thank you for embarking on this journey with me.

As "From Doer to Leader: The Art of Delegating with Impact" finds its way into your hands, I hope it serves as a source of inspiration, guidance, and empowerment. May it empower you to become a delegating leader who not only achieves remarkable results but also leaves a positive and lasting impact on the world around you.

With heartfelt thanks,

Mohd Arif

End Notes

1. Covey, Stephen R. "The 7 Habits of Highly Effective People: Powerful Lessons in Personal Change." Free Press, 1989.

2. Drucker, Peter F. "The Practice of Management." Harper & Row, 1954.

3. Goleman, Daniel. "Leadership That Gets Results." Harvard Business Review, March-April 2000.

4. Blanchard, Kenneth H., and Johnson, Spencer. "The One Minute Manager." William Morrow, 1982.

5. Pink, Daniel H. "Drive: The Surprising Truth About What Motivates Us." Riverhead Books, 2009.

6. Collins, Jim. "Good to Great: Why Some Companies Make the Leap... and Others Don't." HarperBusiness, 2001.

7. Maxwell, John C. "The 21 Irrefutable Laws of Leadership: Follow Them and People Will Follow You." Thomas Nelson, 1998.

8. Grant, Adam. "Give and Take: A Revolutionary Approach to Success." Viking, 2013.

9. Buckingham, Marcus, and Coffman, Curt. "First, Break All the Rules: What the World's Greatest Managers Do Differently." Simon & Schuster, 1999.

10. Charan, Ram, Drotter, Stephen, and Noel, James. "The Leadership Pipeline: How to Build the Leadership Powered Company." Jossey-Bass, 2000.

11. Pink, Daniel H. "To Sell Is Human: The Surprising Truth About Moving Others." Riverhead Books, 2012.

12. Kouzes, James M., and Posner, Barry Z. "The Leadership Challenge: How to Make Extraordinary Things Happen in Organizations." Jossey-Bass, 1987.

13. Blanchard, Kenneth H., Carlos, John, and Randolph, Alan. "Empowerment Takes More Than a Minute." Berrett-Koehler Publishers, 1996.

14. Lencioni, Patrick. "The Five Dysfunctions of a Team: A Leadership Fable." Jossey-Bass, 2002.

15. Maxwell, John C. "Developing the Leaders Around You." Thomas Nelson, 1995.

16. Welch, Jack, and Welch, Suzy. "Winning." HarperBusiness, 2005.

17. Rockefeller Habits. "Scaling Up Business Growth Workshop." https://scalingup.com/

18. Harvard Business Review. "Why CEOs Must Become Chief Delegation Officers." https://hbr.org/2018/03/why-ceos-must-become-chief-delegation-officers

19. Forbes. "The Delegation Playbook for Startups." https://www.forbes.com/sites/forbestechcouncil/2019/05/24/the-delegation-playbook-for-startups/?sh=1680aa5b3e6b

20. Inc. "7 Delegation Strategies for Startups and Small Teams." https://www.inc.com/samantha-harrington/7-delegation-strategies-for-startups-and-small-teams.html

21. McKinsey & Company. "Managing with Consequences: Unleashing the Power of Delegation."

https://www.mckinsey.com/~/media/mckinsey/dotcom/client_service/organization/pdf/sot112_delegation.ashx

22. MindTools. "Delegation: The Art of Delegating Effectively." https://www.mindtools.com/pages/article/newLDR_98.htm

23. Fast Company. "Why You Should Embrace the Power of Delegation." https://www.fastcompany.com/90408968/why-you-should-embrace-the-power-of-delegation

24. Business News Daily. "Delegating Effectively: Tips for Small Business Owners." https://www.businessnewsdaily.com/15055-how-to-delegate.html

25. The Balance Careers. "Understanding the Benefits and Barriers of Delegation." https://www.thebalancecareers.com/benefits-and-barriers-to-delegating-2276097

26. Harvard Business Review. "When to Delegate, and When Not To." https://hbr.org/2003/06/when-to-delegate-and-when-not-to

27. Forbes. "How to Delegate and Get More Done." https://www.forbes.com/sites/johnhall/2016/09/18/how-to-delegate-and-get-more-done/?sh=4f6db17a7a35

28. American Psychological Association. "The Subtle Art of Delegation." https://www.apa.org/monitor/julaug03/subtle

29. CIO. "7 Tips for Delegating IT Work to Up Your Game."
https://www.cio.com/article/3159056/7-tips-for-
delegating-it-work-to-up-your-game.html

30. Project Management Institute. "Delegation."
https://www.pmi.org/learning/library/delegation-project-
managers-key-success-5789

www.ingramcontent.com/pod-product-compliance
Lightning Source LLC
Chambersburg PA
CBHW070926260726
48661CB00003B/839